The Prosperity Principle

Extract the Gold and Make it Good

Athens Rising Publishing House

The Prosperity Principle
Extract the Gold and Make it Good

Copyright © 2023 by Matthew McKenna

All rights reserved. No part of this publication may be reproduced or used in any manner without prior written permission of the copyright owner, except in the case of brief quotations embodied in reviews, commentary, criticism, satire, further development, and non-commercial uses permitted under copyright law.

Published in Canada by Athens Rising Publishing House
All inquiries can be emailed to athensrisingpublishinghouse@gmail.com

Cover image by Refluo of Vectorshock

Library and Archives Canada Cataloguing in Publication

McKenna, Matthew., author
The Prosperity Principle: Extract the Gold and Make it Good

ISBN: 978-1-7387462-0-0

First print edition: 2023
Printed and bound in Canada

Thank you,

To my family, for the lessons and love they've shown me throughout my years.

Dedicated,

To the human spirit and its ability to overcome any challenge set before it.

"And if someone goes through fire for their teaching—what does this prove? Indeed, it means more when one's own teaching comes out of one's own fire!"[1]
- Fredrich Nietzsche

Contents

Introduction 10
   Our Eternal Story 1
   In The Beginning.. 1
   How Did This Happen? 3
   What is Prosperity? 6
   Who am I to Speak of Prosperity? 8

Part I 14
   The Will to Thrive... 15
   Getting Started.. 17
   The True Purpose of Recreation 19
   The Two Doctors.. 21
   The Importance of Being Able to Follow......................... 24
   There's No War Hero Without Trauma........................... 27
   The Show Must Go On.. 28
   What You Sow is Your Life and Death is the Scythe 30
   What is a Human Being According to Greek Mythology? ... 32
   The Caduceus 34
   Mercury and The Meaning of Life: Extract the Gold and Make it Good 37
   Aura of Excellence... 40
   Be Like Water 41
   What Virtues Do You Stand For?..................................... 43
   Warning For Servants of Light.. 45
   Shiva: Creation and Destruction 47
   Why Are You Worried? 51
   The Religious Roots of Star Wars..................................... 53
   Buddhism: The Happiness Hack....................................... 55
   Is Non-Attachment the Coward's Way?........................... 60
   The Necessity of Fear: Symbolism of the Lion in *The Wizard of Oz* 63

Battle of Strawmen: Symbolism of the Scarecrow in *The Wizard of Oz* 64

In Search of a Heart: Symbolism of the Tin Man in *The Wizard of Oz* 65

The Other Side of Happiness: When the Darkness Comes 68

The Cave You Fear to Enter 70

How To Grow: From Pain to Prosperity 73

Death of the Individual: Our Modern Machine 76

Part II 80

Be Wary of Ideology 81

The Value of Truth 86

Value Itself 91

The World on Our Shoulders 92

Tolkien, Gandalf, and Wisdom in Times of Hardship 96

The Stories We Share: Creation From Chaos 99

Problems and Potential 102

Those Who Build and Those Who Destroy 106

Rules For Argumentation: A Guide to Effective Communication 108

The Problem with Politics 110

The Path Forward: Neither Capitalism nor Socialism 114

The Solution to Wealth Inequality & The Key to Maintaining Prosperity 117

The Great Shadow 120

Evil is Not the Problem 122

Let Us Make Each Other's Friend 125

Statues to Virtue and Vice 127

Do we Deserve Freedom? 130

Feelings of Harm and Empathy 132

The Island and the Flood 133

Are You the Hero or the Victim? 136

How to Build a Dynasty 137

The Eternal Elite 142

Anyone Can Become Wealthy 144

- Excellence Over Equality 150
- The Sickness of Safety 153
- Our Species' Top Priority 158
- Why Did Jesus Encourage His Followers to Own Swords? 165
- The Real Hero of Batman: Shutting the Door on Tyranny When the Opportunity Comes Knocking 168
- Blue Zones 171
- A Tribute to Love 173
- Who We Are 175

Part III **178**
- Beginning of Metaphysics 179
- What is Really Real? 181
- Aristotle and Infinity: The Force of God 189
- Why Does Stuff Move? 191
- Materialism is Demonstrably False 192
- Was The Universe Created? 193
- Patterns and Fractals 199
- The One and The Many: Unity and Multiplicity 203
- Possibility 206
- Metaphysics: Matter, Motion, and Mechanics 207
- Existence, Separation, and Anxiety 215
- Immortality: The God Within and The God Without 217

Part IV **222**
- What Are You When You Are No More? 223
- Searching For the Strawman: What God Is Not 225
- The Om 226
- God and gods: The Mutual Truth of Polytheism and Monotheism 228
- Global Theology: Three Types of God 230
- The Transcendent 232

Part V **234**

The Ultimate Aim 235
What are you Building? 237
What is Your Life a Monument to? 240
Mind and Placebo 241
Alchemy and the Elixir of Life 243
Parable of the Sower 244
The Cure For Anxiety 245
Prosperity and Human Flourishing 246
The Altar of Relaxation 247
The Hero's Journey 249
Necessity 251
The Hero's Vow 252

Endnotes **256**

Introduction

Our Eternal Story

We perceive the world through an ancient tale
As we can't help but search for the holy grail,
The philosopher's stone, and meaning of life,
And how to handle sorrow and strife.
When facing hardship and burned by flame,
We look to myth for where to aim.
As stories of old were understood,
Extract the gold and make it good.

In The Beginning

Ask yourself, where are you going? Who do you want to become? What must you do to get there?

Forget everything you think you know about reality. Go into the depths of your mind and connect with your innermost self. There, you will find the answers at the core of your being.

There, exists a world beyond that of our own. A world of beauty, truth, and complexity far beyond our imagination. A harmony of the cosmos within our minds. The world we see is mere shadows of the luminous life force from which all things stem. This is the god found within us, and it is not what you expect. Shed any expectations and simply be present.

We are embarking on a journey to the core of reality itself. The depths of our mind are not to be tread lightly. We are entering into a realm of powerful forces beyond our comprehension.

I will walk this journey with you, my friend. But there will come a point when you must go on alone.

I will take you to the door, but I cannot enter with you. You must go through that door yourself. And you will find only what you enter with.

Our mind can be a scary place. We may not want to be alone with our thoughts, let alone dive into the source of consciousness. But the person you want to become is on the other side of this journey. You are a mighty ship built to confront ocean storms.

Go forward, and fear no darkness.

. . .

You are the culmination of thousands of years of human evolution. You are descended from great kings and conquerors, mighty warriors and heroes. Greatness is in your blood and glory flows through your veins. In your DNA contains the tales of heroes of old. You share the genes of the best humanity has had to offer. You are an unstoppable force, and the world will soon marvel at what you have become.

You've always felt like you were destined to become something great. You are descended from greatness, and to greatness you shall return. How will you embody this greatness that flows through you? How will you act on this potential to bring good into the world? What is the ideal you are striving for?

Go forth and prosper, being a light in the darkness wherever you are.

How Did This Happen?

The roots of this book can be traced to a website I started in the summer of 2021 titled, *Project Genesis*. I had only begun dabbling in writing at this time and was interested in exploring topics that contribute to creation and vitality. The idea was that through investigating the insights of art, science, and mythology, we can extract how to best live our human experience. The mission of *Project Genesis* was to combine philosophical perspectives, psychological tips, and literary insights, among other disciplines, to form a holistic path to one's ideal self.

The Prosperity Principle has grown out of the pursuit of *Project Genesis*. At its core, this book is a project to seek the good in all things, and to seek value from all disciplines and ways of life. The spirit of *Project Genesis* and its multi-disciplinary approach still characterizes this book, with the following topics relating to philosophy, psychology, history, science, economics, religion, mythology, literature, and much more. The goal of *The Prosperity Principle* is to find the best ideas these disciplines have to offer. This is an attempt to extract the best from humanity's work thus far.

I had some ideas (or did the ideas have me?). I wrote them down. I originally had no intention of publishing these writings in a book, but then I noticed they seem to circle around the same idea—an idea that gives rise to prosperity, human flourishing, and fulfillment of the highest order. Perhaps this is an inaccurate description and my bias clouds my judgement. That is for you to decide.

If this is true, that I have stumbled upon something to uplift the human spirit, is it not selfish to keep these writings for my eyes only? If something within these pages can benefit my fellow human, is it not worthwhile to share it with the world?

With that, I'm convinced I should toss what I have to the world, and let the winds take it from there.

...

There are those who do well, and those who do not. What accounts for the success of some but not others?

Those who do well embody a pattern—a pattern that can be observed, noted, and replicated.

The spirit of excellence has lived throughout the tides of history, amid the rise and fall of empires. There have always been great civilizations, powerful nations, and admirable heroes, all unified by the common tie of prosperity.

To understand the patterns of excellence and the principles of prosperity, one must understand reality, and how the world works. Once we understand how the world works, we can use this knowledge to create the best life possible, both for ourselves and for others. This is the purpose of *The Prosperity Principle*.

The Prosperity Principle is about prosperity and human flourishing. Drawing on insights from science, philosophy, and art, *The Prosperity Principle* explores how to rise above any circumstances to attain the highest state of fulfillment and wellbeing for a human life.

Inspired by the study of history, philosophy, mythology, psychology, political thought, religion, and spirituality, *The Prosperity Principle* examines the human experience and proposes a solution to triumph over the challenges of existence.

Within these pages describe the nature of reality and how to act in the world for optimal results. Life is like a game. And if you know the rules of the game, you can play it well.

...

This is a pattern. At the absolute core of your existence, you're always participating in a pattern of something larger. Everything happens according to patterns. This book; you reading this book; the way you acquired this book. Whether by purchase, gift, or accident, it's all patterns. Who you are and what's happening in the world are patterns. Patterns are fundamental to reality.

Some patterns are better than others. The pattern of fulfillment is certainly better than the pattern of misery. The pattern of peace is preferable to the pattern of war. The pattern of goodness is more desirable than the pattern of evil. But what's the best pattern? And how do we experience it?

My aim is to highlight the best pattern and offer a glimpse into prosperity.

What I intend to do is illuminate the patterns of the world for you, dear reader, to extract an understanding of prosperity and human flourishing.

The Prosperity Principle is about prosperity, human flourishing, and the most fulfilling state of human existence.

What is Prosperity?

Prosperity is a feeling—a feeling of connection with the ultimate way to live, or at least moving towards it.

The feeling of prosperity is a feeling of wellbeing and fulfillment recognizable to us all. The feeling of prosperity is good. It is The Good. It is the *most good* thing there is. The feeling of prosperity is the feeling of love, and joy; the feeling of victory and accomplishment; and the fulfillment of our most important ethical objectives. The feeling of prosperity is that of truth, love, goodness, and wellbeing.

Prosperity is also the feeling of harmony and bliss when released from the anxiety of all that hinders us. Though being released from constraint is liberating, it can be overwhelming. Letting go of stress and releasing what we cling to in the world can create the path to both enlightenment (in the Buddhist sense of nirvana) and to nihilism or meaninglessness. But to emerge from meaninglessness and depression, to rise like a phoenix from our deepest feelings of misery and sorrow, we can find meaning in a seemingly meaningless world.

Prosperity is also the feeling of virtue and good action. It is the feeling of success in practical tasks and the satisfaction of high achievement. It is the feeling of doing the right thing or doing something well. Socially, prosperity is the shared anthem of the oppressor and the oppressed. Prosperity is the striving for The Good beyond ourselves.

There's an experience in every being that is Divine. We find it in the emptiness of ourselves, and in the emptiness of the world. An emptiness that is rich with Being. It is that which underlies all things, it is the cause of causality and that which makes possibility itself possible.

This is also the feeling of getting lost in music, art, sport, or any other romantic and blissful experience. It is a Transcendent experience.

The Transcendent is about a feeling of connection to something beyond oneself. It is an experience of "breaking through" and feeling a sense of oneness with all things; a cosmic sensation of love and unity. You dissolve into the patterns unfolding around you, realizing that there is no you, and that you are the patterns. In doing this, you transcend the material world into something beyond it. To a place beyond the dead world of objects to an eternal experiential state of consciousness. A state of being that is always Being even after your particular human being comes to an end. The Transcendent is the ultimate light in the darkness.

When I say prosperity, I mean the Transcendent itself in its most positive sense. The following book illuminates the principles of how we attain It.

Who am I to Speak of Prosperity?

Seriously, who am I to write about this? I'm not qualified as a regular human being to take on this project. I'm just a person.

Do I have the credentials to speak on such a topic?

No.

Am I equipped to know human flourishing and the spirit of prosperity?

Not likely.

Is it presumptuous to think I have something to say worth listening to?

Maybe, since trying to answer questions about life can be arrogant and disingenuous.

So what makes me think I'm remotely capable of titling a book *The Prosperity Principle*?

After all, I'm just a person. A person who's limited, flawed, and prone to error.

But I try to pursue the Truth. That is my promise to you. This is my sacred bond.

I write about things that I think are important. Or at least, this is what I try to do. Some people get it, some people don't. And that's okay. That's what makes a piece of communication personable. I share my observations and articulate my experiences as genuinely as I feel them, and when I get this right, or at least relatable, this creates a feeling of connection to a truth beyond ourselves.

I am not a powerful leader or politician. I am not famous or renowned. I'm not the executive of a company or at the top of my given field. I'm not wealthy. However, I'm young, and not many of us young people are any of these things, nor should we strive to be, if I'm being honest. I'm not blissful nor living in a constant state of enlightenment, though it seems this is an impossible ideal, even for the Dali Lama himself. I'm no stranger to failure, though I've learned how to encounter adversity. Although I'm not immune to stumble and fall, I've understood how to rise from the ashes every time. I'm driven by meaning and purpose, capable of facing the darkness and triumphing over adversity. Most of all, I am fulfilled.

Failure, doubt, loss, suffering. I've known these. Fear, anxiety, misery, and despair. I've looked into their eyes and seen the darkness of the abyss. But through the darkness, I've found a light; an eternal flame available to us all. It's not of my own discovery, but an ancient idea that has been preserved in the patterns of human culture and sewn into the fabric of reality itself.

Success, triumph, fulfillment, and love. I've known these as well. I've seen both sides of the coin we call life, and I've spent an eternity on either side, each side creating the other. Although the dual nature of existence is inevitable, we can travel between both the light and the dark. As the night follows the day, the darkness will come. There is no preventing a trip to the underworld. Although we can't prevent struggle and hardship, we can triumph over it. When suffering takes hold, we can escape its grasp. When the darkness comes, we can harness the light within.

It's crucial to remember that our light won't shine without darkness. Up implies down. Wrong implies right. Good implies bad. And day implies night. Permanently erasing the bad would eliminate the good, since there would be nothing to define goodness against. Opposites imply one another. This is the way of the world.

I do not offer a path to eradicate the darkness, but to dance between the push and pull of life's flow; to walk the narrow rope across the abyss, and to find one's footing each time we fall.

I've been to the underworld, soared through the Heavens, shaken hands with both God and Satan, met the archetypes, gazed into the timeless eternity of awareness built into the structure of reality itself, and saw my reflection staring back at me.

I looked into the eyes of God, and It let me live. Blessed to know Its face yet cursed to never speak of Its form. With my own fingers, I've touched the pillars on which the cosmos is built upon. Yet as I try to articulate its essence, it turns to dust in my hands, and is scattered to the eternal wind only to reform just beyond my grasp.

I've been privileged with the opportunity to love and be loved. To succumb to hate and be hated.

I've been blessed with curiosity and the gift of the gab. I like to listen and learn. Above all, I strive to understand. I've talked with thousands of people, from all walks of life, and had the privilege of learning about their lives. I've seen the world through their eyes and learned their stories. I'm curious, interested in almost everything, and driven to understand all this world has to offer.

Just some other things about me… I try to be observant and notice what's happening around me. I have a loving and supportive family. I've been blessed with some wonderful friendships and relationships throughout my life, providing the privilege to get to know many people on a personal level. I'm a fan of exploring and expanding consciousness through meditation, breath work, and other related hobbies that I recognize make me sound like more of a hippy than I actually am. But don't worry, there are less subversive ways I spend my time. I enjoy learning. I read books, watch documentaries, listen to interviews with experts on various subjects and immerse myself in history, philosophy, religious and spiritual thought, esoteric and secret societies, economic and political thought, quantum and theoretical physics, just to name a few. I've had a strong religious upbringing followed by an intense period of atheist rebellion, kickstarting my obsession with truth and beginning my pursuit of the true nature of reality. Eventually, I made peace with my angry atheism and accepted the nature of reality, dare I call it, God. All these experiences have influenced me and crafted the person I am today. But at the end of the day, that's all I am—just a person.

I try my best to be honest and speak about what I think matters. This is what equips me to take on the endeavour of speaking about prosperity.

As a person, these are my observations of the truth of human prosperity, if such a thing can be known. People can probably articulate it better than I can, especially concerning a topic as lofty as human flourishing and prosperity. If someone can do it better, I welcome them to do so. In fact, I believe many people have done it better already, and I encourage everyone to consider these matters for themselves and pursue them on their own accord. Perhaps there will be errors in what I say. Though I'm diligent and strive for the truth, I've been wrong about many things in the past, and I'll likely be wrong about many more things in the future. Even though I'm prone to error, I feel compelled to contribute my voice to the conversation. Even if this work is a drop in the ocean of human output and overshadowed by other works, then I hope by tossing my voice to the wind that this work is carried to those who were meant to hear it.

I've encountered many teachers on my path, and I've listened. I've seen the world play out around me, and I've learned. I've studied, I've practiced, and I've reflected, then I've composed to the best of my ability what I would offer back to the world.

May those who have ears, hear, and those who have eyes, see. I hope that the ripple effects of this endeavour create a tidal wave of value for all life.

This, is *The Prosperity Principle*.

Part I
The Individual

The Will to Thrive

Unless suicidal, the drive for survival will motivate a living organism.

But not all life is guided by the will to survive. There are those among us who do not merely survive, but thrive.

Surviving, getting by, and simply not dying is the mantra for many. But for those radiating souls who are unsatisfied with the mediocre, theirs is the will to thrive.

To thrive is to triumph. Success, fulfillment, and prosperity of spirit are granted to those who are guided by the will to thrive. Survival is not triumphing. Survival is the slavery one finds in defeat. Survival is not fulfillment. Survival is the avoidance of death and the longing for a life well-lived. Survival is not prosperity. Survival is getting by with enough to not perish. Surviving is not thriving. To survive is to live, to thrive is to live well.

It seems that some people are driven by a light from within—by an internal energy that pushes them far from average. They seek not only to survive, but thrive. They don't want the mundane and "good enough." They aspire towards greatness and aim at the highest state of virtue. These folks are characteristically different. Rather than just working harder or doing better, they seem animated by a different spirit altogether. At the core of their being is a drive for Greatness.

The will to thrive is not a primal urge for victory or domination, but for prosperity beyond oneself. Those driven by the will to thrive have something of the Midas touch, turning everything they encounter into gold—gold in the sense of richness, quality, and excellence. Those motivated by the will to thrive are not concerned with just living, but living well. And not just living well for oneself, but for the wellness of others too.

Individuals who thrive cause their communities to flourish. Communities that flourish cause their countries to prosper. Countries that prosper lift the world to new heights.

Those whose will aims at survival will act to further their survival, but those whose will aims at thriving will act beyond just surviving. The will to thrive is the seed of Greatness.

Why just survive when one can thrive? The will to thrive is available to all if only they advance beyond the will to simply survive. Thriving is opposed to surviving. Whereas surviving is concerned with keeping one's head above water, thriving aims to soar in the sky above.

Thriving, excellence, harmony, greatness, success, fulfillment, high achievement, and the most prosperous qualities of existence are what we can attain only if we set our sights clearly on prosperity and avoid the pitfalls of mere survival. Life can be okay, or life can be better than okay. The choice is yours.

The will to thrive is available to us all. Within us is a motivation—a drive towards a state of being. It's unfortunate that many of us aim at the mediocrity of "getting by" and mere survival. I offer you a vision of what life could be if it were a life of the highest sort—a life of love, plenty, and fulfillment. Such a life is achievable so long as the goal of life is not simply to survive. I invite you to set your sights beyond just survival. I invite you to aim at the highest ideal for life—prosperity.

Getting Started

Mark Twain once said, "The secret to getting ahead is getting started."[2]

All too often we allow our plans or projects to get repeatedly pushed into the background. We justify it to ourselves by saying we're "too busy" or "too tired." Yet we manage to find time to binge that show on Netflix or waste an hour of our life mindlessly scrolling through social media just waiting for that next hit of dopamine.

There are plenty of ways you're wasting time, and you know this to be true. You feel it when you're doing it. Why do we keep lying to ourselves? Let's take just 20 minutes and dedicate that time to some practice or undertaking we want to begin. That doesn't seem like much, right? I've taken showers longer than 20 minutes! I'm sure you have too. If not, then I'm sure you've sat on the toilet using your phone for 20 minutes doing nothing productive. And hey, fair enough, I'm not holding that against you (I've also done that).

But just imagine taking 20 minutes a day and dedicating it towards whatever that thing is you want to start. Maybe it's learning a language, or building a deck, or reading that book, or even writing a book. Perhaps it's something as simple as replying to those emails you've let get away from you or going through that stack of papers on your desk. Just by taking 20 minutes a day over the course of two years is over 243 *hours* of time you can put towards whatever you want. That's over ten days! Or to really put it into perspective, six straight work weeks. Think about how much you can do in this time. If you increase the daily amount of time to one hour, then you have 730 hours (18 work weeks, or four and a half months of working) to put towards whatever it is that you want to do!

You need to start though. You need to actually get down and do it. You don't need to finish whatever it is in one sitting. But how will you ever finish if you don't even start? Perhaps we're afraid of failure so we don't bring ourselves to begin. Can't fail if you don't start… Although never starting is probably a deeper form of failure that stings the longer it ferments. Maybe we don't think we can do that thing, so we never try. We wouldn't want to prove ourselves right that we are too incompetent, stupid, and clearly unfit for whatever project or endeavor we want to begin. Maybe we just like having something to look forward to. Having that project you're "someday" going to start keeps people motivated. But in this case, you're exploiting something that could be pure and wholesome. The fact you're interested in whatever that endeavor is indicates that it's appealing to you. You're interested in it. Odds are, you could derive satisfaction and fulfillment from this. Perhaps you'll even discover a passion of yours.

Is it right to milk whatever this thing is to keep you going from week to week? Just start the thing. Even if you don't have a lot of time, 20 minutes is all it takes. I'm willing to bet that on some days, 20 minutes will turn into an hour. Most things take as long as you let them, and when you organize your priorities to include those things you want to start doing, everything else falls into place around it. You'll always find things to occupy your time and most of them you'll justify as important. Stop lying to yourself. They're not as important as you think they are. And if they are, then they'll get done after your 20 minutes of whatever that thing is. Stop telling yourself "someday" because the last time I checked, "someday" isn't a day of the week. "Someday" will never arrive. Make that day, today. Start that thing, today. Get started, no matter how small the steps you take. That is the secret to getting ahead.

Good luck and happy beginnings to you.

The True Purpose of Recreation

The word recreation is thrown around a lot in our culture. It seems just about everything has a recreational purpose, such as vehicles, sports, drugs, and other activities. But what does recreation even mean? And where does the word come from? As someone who's a bit of a nerd for understanding the history and etymology of words, the answer certainly surprised me. Understanding the origins of recreation can help us reframe our understanding of leisure, allowing us to lead lives of greater fulfillment, productivity, and vitality.

The common understanding of recreation is something done in one's spare time for leisure or fun. But this isn't where the roots of recreation come from. According to the Online Etymology Dictionary, "recreation" comes from the Latin word, "recreare" which means "to refresh, restore, make anew, revive, invigorate."[3] This is very different from mere fun or leisure activities. Recreation in its purest sense is meant to renew one's spirit. Recreation is to recharge your batteries, remake yourself better, to refresh and revitalize yourself!

Things done in our leisure time that leave us feeling weak, tired, miserable, and drained are the opposite of recreation. These activities don't reinvigorate us. They don't help us renew ourselves and feel refreshed to face life head-on. They do the opposite. Inadequate and counterproductive leisure activities often leave us feeling worse than before we engaged in them. I know for myself that when I partake in counterproductive leisure activities that leave me feeling drained, it feels as if I'm suffering from a disease of the spirit.

Funny enough, the root word "recreation" as it appears in Old French and Latin is also used in reference to the "curing of a person" and "recovery from illness."[4] Recreational activities are not just done for fun, but to cure oneself; to become refreshed, renewed, and full of life.

Understanding the meaning and history of recreation can allow us to return to our roots of recreational activities and reflect on how they should make us feel. If your leisure activities leave you feeling tired and drained, just wishing for one more day of your precious weekend so you can stay in bed and sleep, then these activities aren't recreational. Our recreational time should enhance our life, not make us feel worse. Next time you're considering a recreational activity for your leisure time, ask yourself, does it refresh, renew, and recreate yourself into something better? If the answer is no, then this activity is draining, not recreational.

The Two Doctors

There was an old woman who worried terribly about her son. She always wondered if he was safe, and her mind conjured up constant doubts about his wellbeing. Sometimes if he didn't answer his phone or was late to a visit, she would be sent into a frenzy of anxiety and thoughts that he either died or was hospitalized. Eventually she went to the two doctors and explained her situation.

"I hear you loud and clear," said the first doctor. He continued, "I know what will help you." He proposed the idea of a pulse monitoring device that would be activated so long as her son had a heartbeat.

"This way," explained the doctor, "you'll be able to see when his heart is beating. You won't have to worry then."

The second doctor began to speak. "This device doesn't help treat the worr-," but she was cut off as the old woman spoke.

"This will do just fine. I'll take it. Thanks, doctor."

A few weeks later the old woman returned to the two doctors with tears streaming down her face, covered in sweat, and was so out of breath that she could barely speak.

"I'm so worried about my son. Where is he?" she managed to gasp. "The device is not lit up."

The first doctor who recommended the device politely checked over the apparatus. "Ah, it was just the batteries. Here you go," he said as he handed it back to her. "I'll have another one made, and it'll have a much longer battery life. You won't have to worry then."

The second doctor spoke up. "Ma'am, I'd strongly recommend we try-" But she was cut off once again as the old woman replied to the first doctor.

"Thanks again, doctor. You always know how to help."

And just as the first doctor had said, in several days the old woman received a new heart monitoring device with a 30-year battery.

A few weeks went by and then the woman visited the two doctors again. She said, "I'm so worried about my son. I can't sleep. I know this device stays lit so long as my son's heart is beating, but I can't shake the fear that he's still alive but badly hurt with no one to save him. Maybe he's been in a car accident or was beat up and left in a ditch somewhere."

The first doctor replied immediately, "I hear your concerns. I totally understand." He continued, "We'll upgrade the device to function as a highly accurate GPS location tracker. That way as long as you see him moving, you'll know he's safe enough to be mobile. You shouldn't have to worry then."

The old woman thought for a moment as the second doctor spoke. "This isn't an effective plan. We should instead tr-"

"No, this will do," replied the old woman. "Thanks, doctor. You know best." And once more she was on her way.

About a month later, the old woman came back again to the two doctors. "I'm so worried about my son," she began. "Although I know he's still alive and I can see his location, I get so worried when he's not moving. I fear for his safety and I always have to call him only to find out he's standing in line, or waiting at a red light, or just sitting on the couch. But I'm still so worried." She pleaded, "Is there any way we can update the device to help?"

"With all due respect," began the second doctor, happy to get the first word in, "this has gone too far and we need to stop. None of these solutions are actually helping you. They're just managing your symptoms rather than addressing the deeper problem that needs to be solved. Rather than managing your worry, let's find a solution that eliminates the cause of your worry."

The old woman stared blankly at the second doctor, and then looked at the first doctor.

He said, "We'll install a camera so that your device will offer constant video surveillance of your son. You won't have to worry then."

The old woman smiled. "I'll take it. You know best, doc."

And so it was, life went on and the two doctors continued their practice. One offering solutions, and the other masking symptoms with a quick fix.

The Importance of Being Able to Follow

A commander to his recruit: "You want to lead one day? Then learn how to follow."[5]

- *Game of Thrones*, George R.R. Martin

I was reading Sun Tzu's *Art of War* when I encountered an interesting story:

> "When Wu Ch'i fought against Ch'in, there was an officer who before battle was joined was unable to control his ardour. He advanced and took a pair of heads and returned. Wu Ch'i ordered him to be beheaded.
>
> The Army Commissioner admonished him, saying: "This is a talented officer, you should not behead him."
>
> Wu Ch'i replied: "I am confident he is an officer of talent, but he is disobedient."
>
> Thereupon he beheaded him."[6]

- Tzu, Sun, and Samuel B. Griffith. The Art of War. Shelter Harbor Press, 2016. p. 56.

Why was the officer's disobedience grounds for execution? A cynical view may be to condemn Wu Ch'i as being an arrogant and tyrannical leader, not allowing for any act of personal glory beyond his command. But I don't think this is a correct conclusion.

An army is a machine. And in a machine, many individual parts play a small role in the greater whole. The whole can only operate so long as the individuals do their job. When the individuals no longer do their job or lose sight of their role in the greater whole, they become faulty and no longer serve the machine. When the officer lost sight of the greater role, he became a liability to the army.

The author recited this story to reinforce how military doctrine changed from traditional forms of combat to a highly structured and methodical operation of warfare. Objectively speaking, the structured and methodical approach is more effective than traditional modes of combat. However, this can only be maintained by discipline and obedience. If the individual parts do not follow their role or lose sight of the greater whole, then the system collapses.

So, why does this matter?

Well, it's not just an interesting story that highlights the historical shift in Chinese warfare, but this idea reflects a deeper truth of human nature. It's not just in the military where disciplined operational structures exist. This 'command structure' is also found in corporations, education, sports teams, volunteer events, healthcare, and religious groups, among others. Human beings can accomplish greater achievements and overcome unthinkable obstacles when they operate together as a group. This is why humans live together in the first place. It has been said that "Man is a social animal,"[7] and this is by necessity rather than choice.

I know quite a few young people who are as talented as the officer in the story, and equally undisciplined. I hear it all time, and you've probably heard it too when people say, "I don't like being told what to do," or, "I can't work for a boss." Heck, maybe you are that person. But it has to be understood that the alternative is isolation. Who's going to want to employ someone who can't follow instructions? Who wants to work with someone who always acts as an individual rather than a team member? Who's going to associate with someone who has a reputation for acting outside of the rules? If you want to win, then you have to play the game.

This is a hard pill for natural leaders to swallow, but it's the best medicine they can take. If you don't like following orders and being told what to do, you'll have to attain a position where you can give instructions and lead others.

How do you do this? It's pretty difficult to go out there and start something from the ground up. It's possible, but very challenging. A more efficient way to attain a position of leadership is by climbing the ranks of an already existing organization. Demonstrate yourself as someone capable of not just following orders.

But you have to start somewhere, and it's usually at the bottom. A former colleague of mine used to run kitchens and would tell his complaining dishwashers, "You have the most important job here. We need you. Without you, I have nothing to cook with and customers have nothing to eat off of. Do a good job with this and then you'll get into the kitchen." And this is absolutely true with how the world works. At the grocery store where I used to work, everyone started by pushing buggies and following commands. The same is true with every job, organization, and career out there. Start from the bottom, swallow your pride, work your way up, and put your ego aside.

An exchange from HBO's *Game of Thrones* represents this idea well. When faced with this unfortunate reality of starting from the bottom and following orders, Commander Mormont tells the recently recruited Jon Snow:

"You want to lead one day? Then learn how to follow."[8]

There's No War Hero Without Trauma

Within every war hero, there's always trauma.

To face the fire and develop what it takes to come out on the other side, you're going to pick up a few scars along the way.

When passing on the virtue of heroism, the trauma of war is necessarily projected as well. Survivors' descendants not only inherent the behaviours and beliefs that furthered the heroism of their triumph, but they also inherit the scars of war that come from facing the tragedies of this world.

Most people's families can be traced back through wars, social conflicts, and political unrest. People today are not disconnected from the historical tragedies of our past—we come from them. We are shaped by these tragedies. While millions died, the ones that survived are those that produced you.

From a Darwinian evolutionary perspective, you are the result of the very best. Great kings and queens of the past are your direct ancestors. The blood of heroes flows through your veins. The survivors of your culture's past have produced you—all your strength and all your weakness. You've inherited what allowed them to thrive, but you've also inherited the trauma of what had to be done to survive.

Psychologist Carl Jung once wrote, "No tree, it is said, can grow to heaven unless its roots reach down to hell."[9]

The hell in your core is not a deficiency, but the source of your greatness. In the words of Nietzsche, "You need chaos in your soul to give birth to a dancing star."[10]

Nurture your chaos. Forgive your hell. An unbroken chain of life has passed the torch for you to hold high. It's in your blood to triumph and reach new heights. The heroes of old have produced you, but you also carry the weight of their tragedy and trauma. Your darkness is not a unique flaw of your character, but a shadow cast by your light.

The Show Must Go On

Imagine a play where no character took their exit. No bow is taken. No grand finale of a character arc is fulfilled. This seems like it would be a dull production, devoid of the fundamental realization that defines humanity—the recognition of our mortality.

We may mourn those who die and experience sadness in their death, but these emotions ultimately come from the celebration of life. Like the death of a beloved character in a movie or play, our mourning of their death springs from our celebration of their life and what their character represents.

We commonly think of death as an unfortunate end and something to be avoided. But what if death could be avoided? Imagine a story where no one died. No death, no loss, no mourning… and no life.

The best stories are those that cover the full range of our human experience—including death.

Death gives life meaning. Without death, what does life mean? Without darkness, how can we understand light? Without bad, how can we understand good? The same contrast goes for life and death. Both are an empty word without their opposite. We need life to understand death, and death to understand life. The end gives meaning to the present.

And the present is all we have. So why not make the present good?

It seems to me that life is like a grand drama. So many characters and stories playing their parts and shaping the world. History unfolds like a symphony of sound and a beautiful harmony of patterns. The characters may change, but the story remains the same. When we observe human history and the lives of those who came before us, their worries and anxieties seem small compared to the big picture that they were a part of. Whether these characters like it or not, the world goes on and life continues.

In the big picture, what shines through history is the progression and the continuation against the struggles of life. What matters is the courage to stand against the storms of life and continually rise after we fall. The commitment to make life good despite our traumatic past and tragic future is the story of humanity.

This grand play will continue, and you are a character. Soon enough, your time will come to take a bow. Live your life so that in this moment, you will be proud of your performance and the character you've played.

As the world unfolds around you, what character are you playing?

In the words of Walt Whitman, "The powerful play goes on and you may contribute a verse."[11]

What will your verse be?

What You Sow is Your Life and Death is the Scythe

We all recognize the figure of Death—that hooded figure of darkness clutching a scythe—the Grim Reaper. But why is Death depicted with a scythe?

Although it looks sharp and scary, a scythe is not a weapon. A scythe is a farming tool used to harvest grain and grass. So why does the threatening and frightful figure of Death carry a scythe?

Death doesn't come with a sword to kill, but with a scythe to harvest. The fruits of your life and the growth of your fields are harvested by Death. You're not killed by Death, rather, that which you grew is collected by nature and returned to the forces from where you came. Death is not to be dreaded as one fears an enemy who approaches with a sword, instead, Death is to be celebrated as one who gathers the harvest and reaps prosperity.

If your life is the source of prosperity and something to be harvested, why be anxious about death?

Is the farmer fearful of harvesting their crops?

Does the farmer dread reaping the fruits of their fields?

The farmer is eager to reap their harvest as this is the source of their life and prosperity. Just as the farmer reaps the growth of the fields, Death reaps the growth of your life.

Death is not evil. Death does not come to do harm. Death comes to collect and harvest the life which you've grown. Just as the wheat has a purpose beyond its understanding, so is your life sown and reaped in the cosmic story.

Death gathers that which you've grown. Death comes to reap what you've sown. And since the reaper comes for us all, prepare for him a harvest worthy of celebration.

What is a Human Being According to Greek Mythology?

What is a human being? And how were they made?

If you ask modern scientists, they'll give an impressive chronicle of Darwinian evolution through the process of natural selection as an account of the origins of human beings. If you consult the Abrahamic religions, you'll probably hear the story of Adam and Eve, the first people according to Abrahamic scripture. As significant as both these explanations are, I'd like to direct your attention to the ancient Mediterranean. One of the most insightful and little-known origin stories of human beings is found in Greek mythology.

When people think of humans in Greek mythology, they typically recall humanity receiving the gift of fire from Prometheus. What isn't as popular is the story accounting for the creation of human beings.

It is said that "Prometheus molded men out of water and earth." But it was "Athena, who breathed life the clay figures."[12]

Although this may be entertaining as far as stories go, I suspect this story suggests a deeper argument about human nature. The Greeks didn't just create their gods for entertainment, but to account for the natural forces that govern the world. Greek mythology seems to suggest that humans are specifically created by Prometheus and Athena. If the Greek gods are abstract representations of the natural world, why was it Prometheus and Athena who created human beings? And what does this say about how the Greeks understood human nature?

Prometheus was known as the wisest Titan. His name translates to "forethought," and he was able to see the future. He's associated with fire and the scientific advancement of humanity. Prometheus is also symbolic of knowledge, reason, and intellect. With enough knowledge, and through a scientific understanding of the natural world, one might as well have "forethought" as they're able to accurately predict how the world works.

Prometheus is the force that fashioned humanity from the mud. Symbolically speaking, this isn't far off from modern science's material account for human beings arising from nature.[13]

Although Prometheus created humans from clay, it was Athena who gave the breath of life. What does Athena represent? Athena is courageous in battle, but only fights wars to defend the state and home from outside enemies. Athena is the goddess of the city and urban living. She is also the goddess of handicrafts and agriculture. She invented the bridle, which allowed humanity to tame horses, the trumpet, the flute, the pot, the rake, the plow, the yoke, the ship, and the chariot. She is the embodiment of wisdom, reason, and purity. Along with these features, Athena is the goddess of wisdom, courage, inspiration, civilization, law and justice, strategic warfare, mathematics, strategy, the arts, and crafts. There's an underlying essence that these symbols of Athena all share. Essentially, Athena represents the spirit that underlies human civilization.[14]

Now recall the creation of human beings once again. Humans were made from clay by Prometheus and given the breath of life by Athena. Given what both gods represent, this origin story suggests that the essence of a human being is made from the spirits of Prometheus and Athena. Human beings are characterized by our intellectual and rational faculties, and driven by our passions and social impulses that produce human civilization. To be human is to be crafted by Prometheus and receive the breath of life from Athena. Not only does this account from Greek mythology describe what we are, but it also reminds us of what we should strive to be.

The Caduceus

Figure 1: Image by Refluo of Vectorshock.com

What is the caduceus? And why is it on the cover of a book about prosperity and human flourishing?

The winged staff with twin serpents is a widely recognized symbol appearing in the industries of commerce, medicine, and the military. Dating back to ancient Greece, the caduceus was associated with the god Hermes, however the symbolism of two serpents winding around a staff date back several thousand years earlier to ancient Mesopotamia in the year 3500 BC.[15]

The Greek god, Hermes, who was later adopted as Mercury by the Romans, is the god of negotiation, diplomacy, commerce, and exploration. He's also the god of communication, luck, and thievery. As the messenger of the gods, Hermes facilitates communication between both gods and mortals. Hermes also serves as a guide to souls as they venture into the underworld. Hermes is often depicted with wings and holding his staff, the caduceus, as he travels between the Heavens and the Earth.[16]

The caduceus is a symbol of both depth and simplicity. It's composed of three main parts, the wings, the staff, and the serpents.

The wings are probably the most straightforward symbol of the caduceus, representing Hermes' capabilities as a messenger to travel great distances at incredible speeds. The wings themselves also represent flight and transcendence, which is symbolic of Hermes' ability to fly beyond worlds.

The staff is often used for movement, pointing, and as a focus of direction. Hermes is also associated with consciousness and the delivery of divine messages to the attention of human beings. Where do ideas come from when they seemingly appear out of nowhere? Hermes is said to be the deliverer of these messages. In some sense, Hermes is responsible for where our consciousness and attention focus based on the divine messages he delivers.

The serpents are by far the most interesting symbol of the caduceus. Serpents have been traditionally associated with danger, chaos, and the Devil. Often being poisonous and posing a threat to humans, a fear of snakes is one of the most common phobias across the globe. There's a story that accounts for the twin snakes depicted in the caduceus, and the origin of the snakes seems more symbolic than the snakes themselves.

According to a Greek myth, the caduceus was a gift to Hermes from his brother, Apollo. After Hermes transformed a tortoiseshell into a lyre, a Greek musical instrument, Apollo was so enchanted by its music that he gave Hermes the caduceus in exchange for the new musical device.[17] This act of bringing prosperity out of potential in creating the lyre is characteristic of Hermes, and this theme is also present in the origin of the caduceus. Although there are conflicting accounts, the caduceus was said to be created by Mercury when a staff was placed in between two hostile snakes, locking them in a perpetual conflict with one another as they wind around the staff.[18] Along with using its wings to fly, the carrier of the caduceus can use the snakes as a weapon against those at the opposite end of the staff. The serpents, a dangerous and destructive threat of the world, can be harnessed by the staff holder into something beneficial and prosperous. This is the essence of the caduceus.

This act of creating a benefit out of danger and uncertainty is the spirit of Hermes. This is also the common theme between successful diplomacy, exploration, navigation, negotiation, commerce, and thievery. The association of Hermes with these domains was to recognize the shared qualities for success when encountering the dangerous and chaotic unknown. Hermes can be thought of as the spirit that communicates between this world and the Divine. He's the point of connection between the gods and the material world. Hermes is the underlying pattern that creates prosperity from danger and chaos.

It's for this reason that the caduceus is sometimes associated with medicine for its symbolism of transformative benefit from danger and disease. This is not to be confused with the more common symbol of medicine, the Rod of Asclepius, wielded by the Greek god of medicine and healing, Asclepius. Although the Rod of Asclepius is directly symbolic of medicine, the caduceus is the official insignia of the United States Medical Corps, the Navy Pharmacy Division, and the Public Health Service.

Mercury and The Meaning of Life: Extract the Gold and Make it Good

How did the element mercury get its name? And what does it have to do with the meaning of life?

Mercury is a grey-white coloured element that appears watery at room temperature, which inspired its nickname 'quicksilver.' A fascinating application for mercury is its use in gold extraction and mining. When you expose mercury to raw material containing gold, the mercury will extract the gold.[19]

Mercury was likely named by the alchemists who discovered it. The alchemists discovered many of the elements and shaped our foundational understanding of chemistry. Chemistry and much of modern science grew out of alchemy.

Today alchemy is largely written off and discarded as pseudoscience because alchemists were primarily interested in discovering the mythical Philosopher's Stone. This was a legendary substance said to be capable of turning any metal into gold, bringing wealth and prosperity to its holder, and containing within it the elixir of life that would grant immortality.

So why did the alchemists give the element mercury its name? When the alchemists discovered this element that flows quickly and extracts the gold from raw ore, why did they name it mercury?

Before the element was named, only two other things had the name "mercury"—the planet and the god. The element is named after both of them.

Mercury has the smallest orbit in our solar system, so it travels very quickly around the sun. From the perspective of earth, Mercury looks like it's zipping around the night sky when observed over a period of time. The Romans projected their gods onto the stars and the movement of the planets. You might recognize some of these famous Roman gods and planets, such as Jupiter, Mars,

Pluto, Venus, Neptune, etc. Mercury appeared to be travelling quickly through the night sky and moving between many of the other planets (or gods) from the perspective of Earth.

The planet Mercury was given this name because it's based on the Roman god, Mercury (whom is comparable to the Greek god Hermes), who's the winged messenger of the gods. Mercury is known for his fleetness of foot, winged hat, and quickly travelling between the gods and the earth to deliver messages.

So, the element mercury was partially named after the planet and its corresponding god's speed. This makes sense for a substance given the name "quicksilver."

But the element was also named after the god himself and what Mercury represents.

As mentioned before, Mercury is the Roman adoption of the Greek god Hermes, who is the winged messenger of the gods.

The Greeks thought of human beings as playthings of the gods. And they understood the gods not as real people who existed, but more like forces of the world, similar to how we might understand physics or forces of the unconscious. As an example, think of the god of rage and warfare. Ares/Mars wasn't just some guy, but the force of rage, destruction, and the spirit of warfare that can possess all human beings.

Mercury (the god) communicates ideas, feelings, and emotions from the realm of the gods and presents them to you. This is what happens when you realize something or when an idea/emotion becomes made aware of in your mind. You become aware of something as if it's a message delivered by Mercury himself. In some sense, we are condemned to an existence of always receiving messages from Mercury through the form of our conscious awareness and focus. Hermes is said to be the bringer of these messages. In some sense, Hermes is responsible for where our consciousness and attention focus based on the divine messages he delivers. The Greeks thought of Mercury as that which directs our attention and awareness. Our mental faculties and ideas were thought to have a divine origin, delivered from the gods.

In short, mercury (the element) was named after the god who represents something along the lines of what directs human consciousness.

Why was the element mercury named after this idea? Well, the alchemists thought that the physical properties of mercury are symbolic of the human being. Recall mercury's property of extracting pure gold when mixed with raw ore, and recall how the god Mercury represents the focus of human consciousness. Mercury is that which extracts the gold, and *this is the ideal of what it is to be human*. The ideas and abstract thought presented to us by Mercury have the potential to help enable humanity to make life better. We are that which is meant to extract the gold from the raw ore of the world. Any situation, challenge, or circumstance is an opportunity for the human spirit to extract the gold and make things good.

Perhaps the Philosopher's Stone is not a real stone at all, but is a way to live embodying the highest ideal for a human life.

Aura of Excellence

There have always been those who rise from slavery to positions of power and nobility. This is a mark of all human civilizations and inherent to humanity itself.

That which is achieved through Greatness is not obtained arbitrarily. Wealth, power, love, and influence flock to Greatness like a magnet, as the necessary by-product of Excellence. Excellence comes first, like a seed which then grows fruit.

Greatness will not be constrained by one's social position. Greatness will not be restrained by one's external situation. The flame of Excellence will not be extinguished by the limitations of its vessel.

There are those who will create something from nothing and continually rise from their starting station. There are those who turn all that they touch into gold and illuminate the darkness wherever they wander. Although they wander, they are guided by a light from within.

These people have a discernible mark as if touched by Mercury himself. These people have a light that shines through them, a vibration they emanate, characterized by an aura of Excellence.

Greatness is attainable to anyone who strives for it. For Greatness is not given nor granted, but is achieved in the heart of the individual. Like the falling of dominos, one's Excellence from within causes the Greatness of their life.

No matter the darkness, it can be made bright. The darker the darkness, the brighter the light. Excellence can flourish in even the most unlikely soil, and Excellence is the only plant that makes the earth richer by its flourishing.

It has been said that humanity is a rope over an abyss. Instead, humanity is a doorway from which the light of Excellence may shine unto the world.

Be Like Water

In a world that feels increasingly chaotic and unpredictable, we often wonder what this means for our lives. We try to plan for the future and have life figured out, only to have the world change once again beneath our feet.

Most of the products we use today and many of the jobs in our economy didn't even exist just 40 years ago. Given that the world is constantly changing, what works today might not work tomorrow. In fact, it probably won't. As life flows on, our environment changes. And, evolutionarily speaking, death awaits those who don't adapt to their environment.

This begs the question: what should we be if our environment is constantly changing?

In the words of Lao Tzu from the Tao Te Ching:

> *"Men are born soft and supple; dead, they are stiff and hard.*
> *Plants are born tender and pliant; dead, they are brittle and dry.*
> *Thus whoever is stiff and inflexible is a disciple of death.*
> *Whoever is soft and yielding is a disciple of life.*
> *The hard and stiff will be broken. The soft and supple will prevail."*[20]
>
>   *-   Verse 76*

Although the *Tao Te Ching* was written over 2500 years ago and is ignorant of modern scientific knowledge, it provides a timeless insight into the way the world works. That which thrives is that which can adapt to change. Survival depends on adaptability.

This sentiment is also expressed by the martial artist, Bruce Lee:

"Empty your mind, be formless, shapeless, like water. If you put water into a cup, it becomes the cup. You put water into a bottle and it becomes the bottle. You put it in a teapot it becomes the teapot. Now, water can flow or it can crash. Be water, my friend."[21]

Like water, we should strive to become adaptable and able to change with our environment. Psychology tells us that human beings function best with a routine. And history tells us that no routine will last forever. Although human beings are creatures of habit, we must learn to change our habits when they are no longer sufficient. This includes changing our lifestyle, philosophy, and even identity.

When we cling to an identity, it becomes impossible to grow beyond it. Just as we let go of a raft that no longer floats, we must let go of who we think we are when our environment changes. We must be adaptable and flow with life as it unfolds, becoming what we need to be for life to prosper.

Don't run from change and don't let the chaos hinder you. Welcome change as an opportunity for growth and prosperity. When chaos comes, light a torch in its darkness. There is always a way for those who know where to find it.

As the river of history rages onwards, become the water that brings life to wherever it flows. As our environment changes, become that which can adapt. Be that which can thrive wherever you go. No matter where you are or what's happening around you, extract the gold and make things good.

What Virtues Do You Stand For?

I want to raise my glass to celebrate the virtues of humankind, not critique their moral failings. For what a dull life it would be to overlook the light and see only darkness. Sure, this darkness ought to be recognized, but only as a shadow of the ultimate light.

It's not the flaws of people that we should focus on, but on the ideals they embody and the moral virtues they possess.

Where are you aiming? What have you built and what have you done? I do not care for where you stumble, and I'm only interested in your failings insofar as they kept you from the heights which you were striving. Focus on the strive, not the stumble.

Every human being has flaws, but not everyone excels in their virtue. I don't care about what makes you a human, I care about what has made you a god. Excellence of character is much older than our mortal lives. The virtues we admire have been around long before we were born and will exist long after we die. As far as I'm concerned, virtue is eternal. When we express this timeless virtue, we embody the divine force of prosperity that brings light to the darkness.

Although on a practical level, I do care about where you have stumbled. As people of goodwill, we should seek to advise one another and help each other along the way as we strive for virtue and excellence of character. Learning experiences and growth from times when we miss the mark are essential to understanding the Good Life. But on a moral level, I hesitate to judge one's intentions and character based on flaws and wrongdoings. Perhaps it's naive, but I believe most folks' hearts are in the right place, and they're just trying their best given their circumstances.

But the difference between folks is that some people have stopped trying to do their best. They've not only missed the mark, but they've stopped aiming for it entirely. They've lost interest in striving toward goodness and virtue. They've given up their quest for the highest ideal. They've let their worst flaws have their way with them. They provide the sins of humanity with a vessel to release their ruin. Their soulless and cold ecstasy keeps vice in the minds of men and dark shadows in their souls.

Vice and instances of moral failings are to be expected from imperfect creatures. But virtue and acts of moral goodness are the chief aim of analyzing one's conduct and character. To criticize one's conduct without the guidance of The Good is to spite Virtue itself by critiquing its opposite without appealing to the source of all goodness.

The temptation of vice pulls everyone in from time to time, but not everyone strives against it. Not everyone reaches for greatness. Not everyone cares to be better than their worst qualities.

While it's tempting to focus on flaws and vices, we should instead focus on how we attain virtue. For this is the only path to keep the ultimate aim of the Good Life in our sights.

I want to raise my glass to celebrate the virtues of humankind, not critique their moral failings. For what a dull life it would be to overlook the light and see only darkness. Sure, this darkness ought to be recognized, but only as a shadow of the ultimate light.

Warning For Servants of Light

You've heard it said that we should be good—that we should strive to turn all we touch into gold and be a light in the darkness. We are called to bring light into this world.

Though this should be a cause for reflection. Ancient stories speak of another light bringer. His name was Lucifer.

Lucifer was an angel before becoming Satan, the Devil himself. Lucifer means "light bringer" and was the title of God's most trusted and right-hand angel.[22] Lucifer was the most beautiful, intelligent, and glorious of all the angels.

Then he fell.

Lucifer began to think of himself as above God. He started a rebellion in Heaven and one-third of the angels rallied to his side.

They were defeated and were cast out of Heaven. After falling to Earth, these angels became demons.[23]

The irony of this story is that the name "Lucifer" literally means "light bringer." What was Lucifer's fatal sin? What sent the bringer of light into the darkness of Hell?

Pride.

The deadliest of the seven deadly sins. To borrow a thought from the Catholic Theologian, Bishop Baron, pride is an iciness of the soul that makes all things colder.[24]

Lucifer thought he was above the ultimate reality. He thought he was the most high. He thought he was the bringer of light and the origin of light itself. It wasn't enough for him to serve Good; Lucifer thought of himself as The Good.

It would be incomplete to think of the Devil without considering God. God is love, truth, goodness, and the ultimate reality. God is the source of all things and the underlying bedrock that holds reality together. Lucifer thought he was the source of these things, and for that, he was then cast into Hell.

Lucifer is a warning to all those who want to bring light to the darkness. It's important to avoid the Devil and his pride. We must recognize that we are not the source of goodness, but serve a good beyond ourselves.

And this is the Luciferian warning—humility. Be wary of pride and never confuse yourself with the ultimate source of light.

Light is also symbolic of ideas and the intellect. Hence the image of a light bulb over one's head when they have an idea. The relationship between illumination and ideas can be traced back to the ancient Greeks. The Greek word for "idea" is "idein" which means "to see."[25] Oftentimes the intellect can fall in love with itself, getting caught up in ideas of its own creation. It's important to remember that ideas are only seen through a light beyond oneself.

Those who bring light risk misstepping and falling from the heights in which they soar. Those with the light think that they see the truth. When they become prideful and corrupt, they consider themselves above others and think they see more than their neighbours. They become convinced that they are the source of light. They think they hold the keys to the castle of prosperity. Lucifer is the intellect, pride, and the uprising against God himself.

So where does this leave our relationship with light? If the Devil in all his darkness began as the bringer of light, should *we* even bother trying to illuminate the darkness?

Light is not bad because Lucifer fell. Lucifer fell because he thought of himself as the source of the light he reflected. Light is not bad, though we must remember the light beyond us. The light we bring does not come from us, but from the Transcendent beyond ourselves.

Those who bring light must remember that they are not the source of truth and goodness, but are in service to the ultimate light.

Shiva: Creation and Destruction

Figure 2: Photo by Kenneth Lu, changed to black-and-white. To view the original image, visit https://commons.wikimedia.org/wiki/File:Shiva%27s_statue_at_CERN_engaging_in_the_Nataraja_dance.jpg

This is Shiva, the Hindu god of destruction.

It's curious why his statue sits in front of CERN in Switzerland. CERN stands for the French name, Conseil Européen pour la Recherche Nucléaire, in English, European Organization for Nuclear Research, and is an internationally renowned scientific institute. Home of the large hadron collider, CERN leads the world's cutting-edge science on the frontier of human knowledge. So, why is there a statue of Shiva out front practically guarding the entrance?

The conspiracy theorists say it's a message... a secret message from the global shadow government implying the devastating experiments taking place at CERN. The large hadron collider and other pieces of advanced technology could be altering the fabric of reality, manipulating world events, and sending humanity on a course to certain destruction. They say, why else would the god of destruction be featured here? Needless to say, these theories are bullshit.

To continue down this rabbit hole... according to some internet conspiracy theorists, the Mandela Effect, which is the phenomenon of remembering something differently than how it was, is caused by our universe jumping to slightly different parallel universes due to CERN's experiments altering the fabric of reality. Needless to say, this theory is also bullshit.

Let's get back on track. The statue of Shiva was gifted to CERN by the Government of India to commemorate their association in scientific endeavours. This may explain why the statue sits in front of CERN, but why this particular statue? Why Shiva? Why the god of destruction?

What people don't realize is that the Hindu god of destruction is also the god of creation. The ancient Hindus noticed that these two forces were the same thing. Creation and destruction are linked to each another. They are two sides of the same coin.[26]

In this case, destruction isn't necessarily bad, and creation isn't necessarily good. Destruction often implies misery, suffering, and negativity. But some destruction can be good. Like the destruction of cancer cells. Or the destruction of asteroids before they hit Earth. And creation doesn't always mean goodness. Wars can be created. We can also create tyrannical governments and disease.

Although seemingly opposite, creation and destruction stem from the same force. Creation and destruction need one another and always exist together.

When you cut down a forest, you don't just destroy the forest—you create a clearing. When you then build a cabin, you don't just create a structure—you destroy the openness and nothingness of the clearing.

When something is destroyed, something else is created. And when something is created, something else is destroyed. The forces of creation and destruction are connected to one another. They go hand in hand.

The ancient Hindus thought creation and destruction are the same force of the universe and represented them as a god. Hinduism considers Shiva as the life force of the universe, responsible for all creation and destruction.

The common sense idea is to think of creation and destruction as two separate forces. But it's important to remember that they're the same thing. Creation necessitates destruction. And destruction implies creation.

If we want to create something, something else must be destroyed. And if we want to destroy something, then something else must be created. This is just how the universe works.

This can be tremendously beneficial when thinking about creation and destruction in our own lives. The forces of creation and destruction live within us. We are always creating and destroying, and we must be conscious of where this energy is being directed. If we want to become something we're not, then a part of us has to die to make room for this new creation. If you want to be more motivated and productive, then the unmotivated and lazy part of you must be destroyed. If you want to adopt a kinder and more empathetic attitude, then the rude and self-centred person within you must die. If you want to create a spirit of optimism and positivity, then the negativity within you must be extinguished.

It can also be beneficial to recognize our opportunity to create things in this world by acknowledging the link between creation and destruction. In every instance of destruction, there's also creation. In all creation, there must be destruction. Although they exist together, some destroyers neglect their capacity to create. And some creators praise themselves for their ability to bring forth new life, while they fail to recognize the destruction in their ways. In your acts of creation, be mindful of your destruction. In your acts of destruction, realize the opportunity for creation. For both go together, as two sides of the same coin.

So why does CERN, a centre for human knowledge and advancement, have a statue of Shiva? Because the forces represented by Shiva are fundamental to the our universe, underlying all instances of creation and destruction. As beings who seek knowledge, understanding, and scientific innovation, we would be wise to remember the forces that govern our development, and harness them to our advantage.

Why Are You Worried?

What troubles you? What disease plagues your mind? A sickness is an accurate way to think of worry. Worry is a dis-ease of the mind. Do you not want to be cured? Do you not want to wash away your worries?

Our tendency to worry stems from something productive and beneficial to our species. Throughout our history, there have always been problems. Death, disease, conflict, betrayal, vicious animals, and cruel neighbours are all problems that the mind must face. Our mind has evolved to solve problems. Those who could not solve problems did not survive to pass on their way of thinking. Our ability to worry and solve the problems we face is what has elevated our species to the heights we occupy today.

However, the exceptional problem-solving ability of the human mind can betray its master. It has been said that anxiety is the ability of the human mind to solve problems of the future. We've gotten so good at solving problems that we stress about things that haven't happened yet, and might not happen at all.

Remember, worrying originated as a productive use of brain power to solve problems. The following flow chart reminds us how to be productive with our thoughts and avoid the unhelpful pitfalls of worrying.

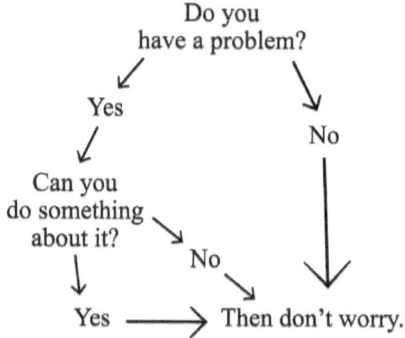

Figure 3: Image not of my own creation. It was shared by an anonymous user on the internet forum, Reddit.

What's the issue? Is this problem within your control? Most importantly, can you do something about it?

If you can't do something about it, then don't worry about it. It's a waste of time to worry about something out of your control. Thinking about it will not help you. Nothing you do will affect the issue. Focus your mind on other thoughts that will be more fruitful and beneficial.

If yes, and this problem is within your control, then do something about it. Instead of thinking about it, realize that you can do something about the problem instead of worrying.

Either way, it's a waste of time and energy to worry. Either you're thinking about something that is outside of your control, or you're wasting time thinking about something within your capacity to change. Don't worry, go do it. If it's out of your control, then let it go.

The Religious Roots of Star Wars

Although Yoda is a *Star Wars* fan favourite, few people are aware of the character's inspiration. According to George Lucas, the film's writer and director, Yoda's character was profoundly influenced by a Buddhist monk he met while traveling in India prior to filming *Star Wars: A New Hope (1977)*.[27]

But is that where the Eastern influence ends?

Yoda's character isn't the only aspect of *Star Wars* that was influenced by Buddhism. Many of the film's most iconic ideas, such as the Jedi Order, Sith Lords, and the mystical Force have their roots in Buddhism and other Eastern religions.

Beyond the spaceships and lightsaber battles, The *Star Wars* films have a distinct religion and present a conception of the ultimate reality—the Force. The Force is described as, "an energy field created by all living things. It surrounds us and penetrates us; it binds the galaxy together."[28]

The idea of the Force is very similar to the Eastern idea of the Tao (the yin/yang symbol), which is described by Taoist scholars as, "the organic order underlying and structuring and pervading all existence." However, this definition doesn't fully encapsulate the essence of the Tao, as it is beyond the limitation of words and is often translated as "eternally nameless," and "that which cannot be named."[29]

In the *Star Wars* universe, being able to tap into the ultimate reality and "use the Force" is a powerful ability. It unlocks the ability to move objects without touching them, read minds, and accurately predict the future, among other capabilities. Accessing the Force is done through mindfulness and meditation, a central practice in most Eastern religions. Meditation can allow one to access their true self and ascend to a higher state of consciousness known as enlightenment. It is enlightenment that connects oneself to the ultimate reality.

Just as the Tao is symbolized by notions of light and dark, so is the Force. People sensitive to the Force usually fall into two categories—the Jedi, who access the light side of the Force, and the Sith, who use the dark side of the Force.

Let's start with the Sith. The Sith are always the bad guys in the *Star Wars* movies and represent the dark side of the Force. They're usually tyrants dressed in all-black trying to blow up planets, murder innocents, and gain unlimited power. Some can even shoot lightning from their fingertips. If you haven't caught on, they're categorized by negativity and bad vibes.

Yoda offers some insight into the dark side of the Force, saying, "Fear is the path to the dark side. Fear leads to anger; anger leads to hate; hate leads to suffering."[30] The Buddhists would say that the root of fear is desire. In fact, Buddhism believes that desire, clinging, and craving are the root of all suffering.

The Jedi on the other hand, represent the light side of the Force and have been described by the creator of *Star Wars* as being, "warrior-monks who keep peace in the universe."[31]

What differentiates the Jedi from the Sith? Eastern religions would say the difference is found in one's relationship with the Tao (or the Force). From the perspective of Eastern religions, desire and craving keep the Sith in the cycle of suffering, called samsara, while the Jedi "let go" by extinguishing their desires, which ends their suffering, and allows them to attain peace, enlightenment, and nirvana.

Buddhism: The Happiness Hack

Buddhism is interesting in that it's one of the world's largest religions while not being an actual religion. Buddhism is more of a lifestyle and a philosophy. While there's some variety across different Buddhist schools of thought, Buddhism doesn't require the belief in an afterlife, following commandments, or even faith in a god. Buddhism at its most fundamental level is to follow the teachings of the Buddha on one's path to enlightenment.

Buddha comes from the word "buddho" meaning "awake."[32] The story goes, that before the Buddha was *The Buddha*, he was a prince named Siddhartha Gautama who lived 2,500 years ago. Upon his birth to a mighty king, Siddhartha's father invited priests to a feast at his palace to celebrate the prince's birth and predict his future. The priests concluded that Siddhartha would become a great and powerful ruler over all the land, or he would become a great spiritual teacher.

Wanting his son to become a powerful ruler instead of a spiritual teacher, the king kept Siddhartha inside a walled palace complete with everything a human being could ever desire. Up until he was a young man, the prince was surrounded by gorgeous gardens, delicious food, luxuries of all kinds, and only beautiful young people for him to see. The prince was kept in the lavish palace to prevent him from ever seeking a world beyond his luxury. To ensure he would not be drawn to any distracting spiritual pursuits, the palace was kept free from sickness and death, leaving only perfection to occupy the prince on his path to becoming a powerful ruler.

Siddhartha begged his father to see the world outside the palace, and eventually when the prince was a young man, the king gave in. He arranged for an escort to take the prince outside the walls. On his journey, the prince spotted an old decrepit man, the first he had ever seen. He asked his escort, "What is this man?" to which his escort replied that this was an old man and that everyone would age someday, even the prince. This troubled the prince, and he fled back to the palace. Someday he would become an old man, and this pained him greatly.

The second time Siddhartha ventured outside the palace, he saw a sick woman suffering from a disease. When asked "What is this?" his escort told the prince that this was a person suffering from disease and sickness, and that everyone would suffer this fate, including him. The prince was troubled by this discovery and returned to the palace. The realization that he too would suffer disease caused him distress.

Eventually, the prince left the palace a third time and discovered a corpse. When asked what it was, his escort told him that this was a person who had died and that everyone would meet this end, even the prince. This troubled the prince so greatly that he returned to the palace.

No matter how many luxuries he distracted himself with, the prince could not stop thinking about the inevitability of old age, disease, and death. Try as he may, the prince knew he could not avoid these fates. Later, the prince left the palace once again. This time he discovered a wandering ascetic with a shaved head wearing a bright yellow robe. When asked what he was doing, the ascetic told the prince that he had renounced all worldly possessions, and this brought him peace. The prince returned to the palace and continued to suffer from the thoughts of old age, disease, and death. But his thoughts would often return to the ascetic who claimed to attain peace.

Eventually, the prince escaped the palace in pursuit of spiritual liberation. After joining a group of ascetics and trying unsuccessfully to attain enlightenment, Siddhartha sat under a Bodhi tree and vowed he would not get up from meditation until he attained enlightenment.

While meditating, Siddhartha realized that everything changes, everything is impermanent, and everything is interconnected. He also realized that our desire for the world to be other than how it is, causes us to suffer. To become liberated from this suffering is to detach from our desire. In the midst of enlightenment, or nirvana (which translates as "to extinguish" or "to blow out"), Siddhartha awakened, becoming the Buddha. He would go on to share these teachings with the world and spawn a philosophy that would change the course of human history.

At the core of Buddhism is the concern with suffering. At the deepest level of human existence, we suffer. This is the problem the Buddha wanted to address, and Buddhism seeks to overcome the suffering of the human condition. In fact, when asked by students about metaphysical questions of an afterlife, God, or the nature of reality, the Buddha refused to comment, saying that speculation of these topics was not conducive to liberation and the cessation of suffering. Instead, the Buddha chose to discuss the mind, desire, and our relationship with pain and suffering.

From the Buddhist perspective, we suffer because we desire and cling to things. For Buddhists, suffering is understood as desire, clinging, or craving. Most of the time, we suffer because the world is different than how we want it to be. Something causes us suffering only when we want it to be otherwise. But if we stop wanting something to be other than how it is, then we don't suffer for it. Oftentimes our suffering isn't caused by a particular thing, rather our suffering comes from our desires about that particular thing. In these cases, suffering is based in the mind. Buddhists think that once we remove our desire, then our suffering disappears as well.

Consider the following examples. The person who craves designer clothes or fancy cars suffers when they don't have these things. When their desire is left unfulfilled, they suffer. Or when these lavish things are damaged, they suffer. But if they remove their desire for these things, then their suffering disappears as well. For example, if someone no longer *wants* their car to be perfect and without dents, then they won't feel anguish in the event their car gets dented. Or, think of a person who desperately wants a promotion at work.

They crave this promotion and this causes them to be unhappy so long as they don't have it. They cling to the idea that they must get this promotion in order to be fulfilled. But if this person stopped desiring a promotion, their suffering over not obtaining it would stop as well. The lack of a promotion isn't bad in itself, it only becomes bad when we want it to be different than how it is. When we suffer with our relationships, with work, with the prospect of old age, disease, and death, we suffer because the world is often different than how we would like it to be. But once we remove our desire for the world to be different from how it is, then our suffering disappears. Once we "extinguish" or "blow out" our desire, our suffering disappears, and we attain nirvana/enlightenment.

This is the fundamental idea of non-attachment. If you can detach your desire from the world, then you'll never suffer from the way the world is.

It seems that Buddhism has discovered a back door hack to the psychology of happiness and the alleviation of suffering. Followers of Buddhism are able to alter their feelings of pain and suffering by consciously letting go of their desires. Since our feelings of pain are linked to desire, Buddhism suggests we should dispense with our desire to be free from our pain. From this perspective, detaching from desire is the path to liberation.

Over the years, some schools of Buddhism have taken on typical characteristics of organized religion. Dogma, doctrine, and metaphysical beliefs have found their way into the teachings of Buddhism. Though it's important to remember that anything aside from the liberation from suffering is not core to original Buddhist thought.

Since Buddhism in its pure and original form focuses on the liberation of suffering, it has garnered the interest of people around the globe, especially people from North America and Europe where organized religion has seen a decline over the past decades. The version of Buddhism that focusses on the problem of human suffering is simple, appealing, and less reliant on believing things on faith like most religions have with their belief in a god, an afterlife, and other doctrines that may be harder to accept. As was the case thousands of years ago, the problem of suffering still plagues the human mind, and Buddhism offers a solution to the pains of existence.

Is Non-Attachment the Coward's Way?

It has been said that letting go of our desires is the path to liberation from suffering. It seems that attachment and desire are the cause of suffering, which is why some philosophies like Buddhism and other attitudes of non-attachment encourage people to detach from their cravings, clinging, and desires. While non-attachment may prove effective at reducing our suffering, should the reduction of suffering be our ultimate goal? Is it not cowardly to live a life free from suffering at the expense of our desires? Are there not desires worth suffering for?

Buddhism and philosophies of non-attachment act as a back door hack into the human psychology of happiness. We eliminate our suffering by eliminating our desire, craving, or clinging. When the world is different than how we want it to be, we experience pain. This is a valuable insight into the cause of suffering. It is important to know why we suffer so we can reduce our suffering when it is unnecessary.

But perhaps suffering shouldn't always be avoided. Perhaps sometimes suffering is necessary. Although we can eliminate our suffering by removing our desire, perhaps there are things worth suffering for. While the elimination of our suffering is tempting, a life aimed at the elimination of suffering entirely neglects the valuable goods that are worth their suffering to achieve, such as human flourishing and the prosperity of our community.

Should our goal be the alleviation of suffering, or the creation of prosperity? Although desire leads to suffering, it seems some desires are worth suffering for. Some goals are worth their pain to achieve. Some labours justify their suffering through the good they create. Peace can be difficult to achieve, but it is nonetheless valuable. Freedom and opportunity are worthwhile desires, though they cause suffering through their pursuit. The prosperity of human civilization is sometimes a painful endeavour, but it is nonetheless a goal we should strive for even if this striving causes us to suffer.

It's cowardly to avoid suffering at the cost of excellence. Do we not have a duty to better this world? Is the betterment of humanity and ourselves not a worthwhile endeavour? When the night comes, are we not called to be a light unto the darkness? Or is human flourishing achieved in darkness by not desiring the light? If one doesn't desire light, they cannot suffer for it. But light can be found in darkness. And it seems that the goodness of the light is self-evident. Goodness, flourishing, and human prosperity justify themselves. Are these goals not worth suffering for? Is this suffering on behalf of goodness not the meaning that we crave? Is the absence of suffering comparable to human flourishing and the highest form of fulfillment? Buddhism and theories of non-attachment offer a path out of suffering. But there is an alternative path—a path into prosperity.

Gordon Allport famously said, "To live is to suffer. To survive is to find meaning in the suffering."[33] Non-attachment and pursuits that eliminate our suffering focus on the suffering rather than one's sense of meaning. A life of extreme non-attachment doesn't seem like much of a life. It seems like a sterile and empty alternative to the pains of existence. Of course, Buddhists will say this emptiness *is* the aim. But perhaps it isn't. Perhaps we should aim at a better world even if this aim causes us to suffer. We should desire, strive, and suffer for a vibrant and prosperous world rather than abandoning the striving altogether for an empty bliss. Through non-attachment, prosperity can be found in our own minds. But through our striving, we can bring prosperity into the world.

Some say this lifestyle is futile since problems are inevitable. They'll keep popping up. Critics will say that problems are like the mythological Hydra—you cut off one head and seven more will grow. Buddhists and Eastern thought suggest we should embrace problems as an essential feature of reality and let go of our desire to alleviate them. Extinguish our desire like blowing out a candle, and the cessation of our suffering will follow. But this doesn't make life better. It hacks our mind to not suffer from the problems of life, but refusing to solve problems in the world allows problems to grow. Although all our problems will never be solved, individual problems *can* be solved. We are the kind of beings who can do this. To neglect our ability to solve problems in the world is to reject our obligation to make life better.

Letting go of some desires can be helpful to eliminate unnecessary suffering. But some things are worth suffering for. Peace, love, enlightenment, human flourishing, and global prosperity seem like ideals worth suffering for. To let go of our desire to make life better so we don't feel bad sometimes seems like the path of a coward. This seems like a justification for complacency, a justification for weakness and laziness in not striving to make the world better. This seems cowardly. Life won't be perfect, but it can always be made better. All problems in the world hold within them the potential for betterment. Addressing the problems of the world is how we make things better. This is what human beings do. This is what human beings have done throughout our history. And this is what human beings will continue to do if they want to live a meaningful and fulfilling life.

The Necessity of Fear: Symbolism of the Lion in *The Wizard of Oz*

It's interesting how in *The Wizard of Oz*, the lion is a cowardly character and searches for courage even though lions are commonly associated with bravery. Why would a lion search for courage if that's what a lion is supposed to represent? Why would this lion lack courage when it's supposed to be the pinnacle of bravery? I think the answer is best framed through a question: Is a lion courageous if it never feels afraid?

Of course not. Because come on, it probably doesn't feel fear. Why would something so strong and fierce get scared? And if a lion doesn't feel fear, then it seems strange to say that a lion is courageous.

After all, there's nothing courageous in doing something that doesn't scare you. Courage is not the absence of fear, but acting in spite of fear. Fear is necessary for courage. You need to be scared to actually be courageous.

Not to mention, why would a lion even need courage in the first place? It's just biologically superior to the rest of the food chain (except groups of humans). The lion is a quintessential apex predator. So where's the room for courage when nothing scares you? Well… there is no room for courage. The lion lacks courage.

We all want to be courageous. We regularly hold ourselves back because of fear and wish we weren't so scared. But *The Wizard of Oz* seems to suggest that being a lion will still leave us as cowards searching for courage. Courage is to be found in embracing fear and acting in spite of it anyway. It's tempting to think that being courageous is to be a lion without fear. But true courage is through fear and can only be found in fear.

We should know fear. We should be *okay* with fear. Not just okay with accepting fear, but okay with embracing fear! We should walk the path of fear like it's the road to victory. So long as we're lions, we can never be fearful. And so long as we're not fearful, we can never be courageous.

Battle of Strawmen: Symbolism of the Scarecrow in *The Wizard of Oz*

There's a reason *The Wizard of Oz's* Scarecrow didn't have a brain. He's a scarecrow, also called a strawman.

Okay great, so what is a strawman and what does it have to do with not having a brain?

A "strawman" is a term used in argumentation and occurs when a point or idea is misrepresented to be weaker than it actually is. A "strawman" makes an idea appear weaker and turns it into a hollow and empty vessel. It becomes a fake representation of something else, making the idea easier to refute. Doing this in an argument or debate is called "straw manning" someone's argument, and is condemned as being an irrational fallacy and lacking intellectual integrity.

In *The Wizard of Oz*, why doesn't Scarecrow, the strawman, have a brain? Because living as a strawman is akin to being foolish. When you constantly strawman all views that disagree with your own, you see the world as a cornfield full of strawmen. Perceiving the world in such a way that you don't take opposing views seriously and you dismiss good points without properly engaging with them is to be a living strawman in the cornfields of this world. You become a strawman yourself, and to live this way is to not use your brain.

I can't think of a better way to symbolically represent a character who lives their life as a constant strawman than a scarecrow without a brain. Perhaps this isn't the true meaning behind the character, but it's a fascinating coincidence from which we can extract a timeless truth. Once we start using our brain and take opposing views seriously, we are no longer a strawman.

In Search of a Heart: Symbolism of the Tin Man in *The Wizard of Oz*

The Tin Man completes the trio of Dorothy's entourage in *The Wizard of Oz*. Accompanying a brainless scarecrow and a lion who lacks courage, the Tin Man has a limitation of his own—he searches for a heart.

But why is this? Why does the Tin Man lack a heart?

Made of metal from head to toe, the Tin Man is a symbol of the times. Written in 1900 by L. Frank Baum, the Tin Man seems to represent the industrialization of human work. After industrialization, the skilled craftsman was replaced by legions of factory workers and the artisan was replaced by automation. The industrialization of the human species has come for all. Even the Tin Man's axe is made of metal, as a telling reminder that nothing of a humans' working life can escape the cold and metallic move to industrialization.

The dawn of modern industry revolutionized the world, and we continue to hear its echoes today. More than ever, we inhabit a world of machines. Automation, computers, and technology dominate our lives, with their conquering control and calculation.

Not even humanity's oldest tasks are safe from the spread of industry, replacing the flesh of the woodcutter with metal and machine. So mechanical in its movements. So cold in its calculations. Devoid of life in the most fundamental sense. Machines are dead, lacking the essential qualities of life and passion. Humanity itself has become a machine in desperate need of a heart.

The Tin Man longs to feel again. He longs to be a creature of the heart rather than the mind. The mind of humanity has created technology so productive and efficient, yet hollow to the core. Robots, automation, and machines are essentially lifeless, following the programming and designs of their creator. There's no room for life or for passion. There's no room for the modern industrialized human to feel a connection to their work. The human heart has been removed from work, and the Tin Man searches to fill the void.

The Tin Man speaks to the alienation human beings have experienced with their work since the industrial revolution. Before the rise of automation and industry, the craftsman found himself in his work. The detail, precision, and beauty shined through even the simplest items like chairs and dishware. But with the advent of machines and automated production, humans have been disconnected from their work and alienated from the meaning we once found through our creation. The Tin Man seems to speak to humans' separation from their work, causing our creations to be cold and empty rather than coming from our passions of the human heart. Industry and machines are the work of the mind, causing the human heart to take a backseat.

It's interesting how in Tolkien's *The Lord of The Rings*, the orcs are the only species that use machines and industry. The orcs are ruthless, destructive, and ravage the earth of its resources to fuel their brutal war machine. Influenced by his experience fighting in the trenches of World War I, the first time human combat became industrialized with the creation of machine guns, tanks, and poison gas, Tolkien saw humanity's embrace of modern machines and industry as a loss of our humanity itself. The human heart was taken out of war. Where men had once looked each other in the eyes when they killed, now thousands could be murdered at the hands of a machine. Men became animals, slaughtered without thought or feeling, tools of the heartless war machine.

Humanity is a passionate and emotional being. We experience fear, hope, and beauty. We love, we hate, and most of all, we feel. Machines don't feel. Machines are driven by programming instead of passion. They are slaves to the whims of their masters. Now the Tin Man sees that the overwhelming industry and machinery have consumed the human soul, emphasizing the cold calculation of the mind over the warmth of the heart.

In the words of Charlie Chaplin concerning humanity's move towards industry and machinery, "We think too much and feel too little."[34] This is more evident today with the creation of computers, smart phones, and personal devices. The modern world lives in a digital and mechanized world, divorced from the passions of nature and the feelings of our hearts. Many of us have become like tin men, lacking a heart, longing for a time before machines stole the warmth of the human soul.

The Other Side of Happiness: When the Darkness Comes

We can't have light without darkness
Can't grow flowers without rain
We can't know good without bad
Can't know pleasure without pain

Good entails bad. We can't run from it. Running from the unpleasant side of life is like running from our shadow. We can move as fast as we can and do everything in our power to be in a different position, but our shadow will still be with us. The shadow of life still looms wherever we go.

And this is okay. Shadows are cast by light. And if there's always a shadow, there must be an eternal light to cast that shadow. This duality is fundamental to the cosmos and ought to be embraced.

The darkness necessitates the light. As the *Tao Te Ching* observes, opposites entail one another, necessitating each other's existence. Just as up implies down, good implies bad, and big implies small, so does emptiness imply wholeness, darkness necessitates light, suffering implies fulfillment, and misery implies joy.[35]

This presence of darkness entails the existence of an eternal light. So when the darkness has found you and wrapped your being in its emptiness, embrace it as proof of the light. Find the light through the darkness, because without darkness, there is no light.

In this darkness, the winds will blow and the storm will rage against that which you've built. You'll cling to your support when the fury rains down upon you and you'll wonder if it will ever end—and if it is even worth it to continue on. But this too will come to pass. The darkness will turn to light. The day will conquer the night. The rains will pass and you'll emerge from the storm stronger than you were before.

Or, the darkness may be calm—too calm. A calm that is subtle and empty, causing you to feel hollow and robbing you of any feeling at all. In these moments you may wonder if you will ever feel again, but this too will come to pass.

The darkness is going to come whether you like it or not. Suffering is inevitable. There will be hard times. It will storm, and it will storm hard. The question is not how we escape the storm, but rather, how we withstand it. How will you respond to the storms of darkness? Even in the hard times, ask yourself—what would the person I want to become be doing right now? And then go do it.

The Cave You Fear to Enter

"The cave you fear to enter holds the treasure that you seek."[36]
— Dr. Joseph Campbell

"in stercore invenitur—it is found in filth."[37]
—Dr. Carl Jung

"King Arthur's knights sit at a round table because they are all equal. They set off to look for the holy grail—which is a symbol of salvation, container of the "nourishing" blood of Christ, keeper of redemption. Each knight leaves on his quest, individually. Each knight enters the forest, to begin his search, at the point that looks darkest to him."[38]
— Dr. Jordan Peterson

It is by venturing into the underworld, full of its darkness and adversity, that we can rise above these challenges and emerge from the depths more whole than when we descended. Within the cave we fear to enter, we find that which we most need.

It is through facing our fear that we become what we need to be. Being scared of something highlights our limitations. Perhaps this limitation is justified, such as fearing a physical threat like a bear or a nuclear explosion. But oftentimes this limitation is holding us back from our true potential, such as going outside of our comfort zone, engaging in difficult conversations, changing careers, or being true to others and ourselves. It is through venturing into the cave we fear that we find what we most need. We find ourselves, or better said, we find the part of ourselves that we've been missing, or not yet actualized. Perhaps it is something about us that must be added. Perhaps it is something about us that must be discarded. Either way, in this cave we fear to enter we find the truth of our being.

You're right to fear what's in this cave. It will be uncomfortable. You will face fire and fury. You will be harmed, and you will know pain. You will suffer. You will learn things about yourself that will hurt you. You will face the devil himself, only to see your own reflection looking back at you.

It is only through knowing the darkness that we can find a light to overcome it. It is through doing that which makes us uncomfortable that forces us to expand ourselves and grow in our capacity to encounter adversity. This is what you gain from the cave you fear entering. Most importantly, you emerge from the cave knowing you can triumph over it.

The timeless theme of facing the darkness is emphasized in the work of the psychologist Carl Jung. He argues that by going into the underworld or venturing into our unconscious mind, we encounter our Shadow. Our Shadow is our repressed and undesirable qualities that don't match our ideals. Although uncomfortable, our Shadow is part of us. Wherever we go, our Shadow will follow. Jung suggests that if we continue to repress our Shadow and fail to integrate these qualities into our personality, then our mind will be unbalanced and plagued by neuroticism and projection. The solution is to not eliminate our Shadow and grow beyond its flaws, but to integrate our Shadow into our personality.[39] Facing the darkness in ourselves is how we grow and become more whole. In the words of Jung,

> *"There is no light without shadow and no psychic wholeness without imperfection. To round itself out, life calls not for perfection but for completeness; and for this, the "thorn in the flesh" is needed, the suffering of defects without which there is no progress and no ascent."*[40]

The human mind will always be plagued with a "thorn in the flesh" according to Jung. There will always be some problem or issue that we're experiencing. The solution to these problems is often found in the places we least want to look.

Also in the words of Jung, "One does not become enlightened by imagining figures of light, but by making the darkness conscious."[41]

So I encourage you, don't fear entering this cave. You will survive. Fear not entering this cave because you will miss the opportunity to become more than what you are. The version of you that emerges from the cave is more whole than the version of you that entered. Encountering the challenges in the cave is what makes us more than what we are—it is what makes us whole.

This is an idea represented in the oldest stories of human civilization. On their journey, the hero must descend into the underworld, or travel to Hell. Sometimes this is a literal cave. Other times it's a journey into a social underground. Yet other times, it's a journey into a realm of darkness and shadow.

Within us is our own shadowy underworld as well. It is in this world where we keep our repressions and fears, our insecurities and traumas. This is where we lock up our demons and shield the world from ever laying eyes on the worst that lies within us. This part of ourselves is so terrifying that we often refuse to acknowledge it. We ignore this part of us at our own peril.

This part of us is important. It is a part of us whether we like it or not. If we chose to never venture into our own underworld and face the monsters in our depths, then we will never be equipped to encounter the caves and monsters of the real world. Once we enter the depths of the cave, we can only go upwards. Acknowledging this part of us, making peace with it, and then integrating it in a healthy way is what makes us psychologically whole.

How To Grow: From Pain to Prosperity

"If you have your why for life, you can get by with almost any how."[42]
- Friedrich Nietzsche

A bone that's broken fuses stronger than before. A strong muscle has been torn and pushed to its limits. The person who stands in the triumph of victory has stumbled more times than can be counted.

Everyone wants growth. But not everyone wants to put in the painful work required for growth. Failure, pain, and discomfort are necessary for growth. These are our greatest teachers, and without them, we would not rise from the ashes of what we were to become what we could be.

Growth through pain and discomfort seems to be a recurring theme throughout reality. As mentioned before, once healed, a broken bone is stronger than before. For a bone to become stronger, it must be broken.

This principle is also the core of bodybuilding and muscle growth. Physiologically speaking, "working out" a muscle causes microscopic tears in the muscle fibers. When the muscle heals and these tears are repaired, the muscle becomes larger and stronger than before.

We see the same concept even in nature with forest fires. Forest fires aren't always bad. Once in a while, forest fires are desirable for a healthy forest. When forest fires are delayed or prevented, dead wood and underbrush accumulate over time. In the event of a fire, this build-up of deadwood causes the flames to burn so hot that the forest's topsoil is destroyed, allowing nothing to grow. To prevent these devastating fires that destroy a forest, small fires are a preventative measure while returning nutrients to the soil. For optimal forest health, the burning of deadwood is desirable and has been nature's way for millions of years.

This theme of life through fire is represented in the ancient symbol of the phoenix, tracing its history back to ancient Egypt several thousand years ago. The phoenix is a mythical bird that burns into flames upon death and is reborn from its ashes. The phoenix represents transformation, rebirth, and resurrection. What's special about the rebirth of the phoenix is that it needs fire. The phoenix dies and rises again from its ashes. The phoenix is broken and is remade better than before. It is through the flames of pain and adversity that we rise and are reborn into something new. The phoenix echoes the timeless principle that growth is achieved through the fires of struggle and adversity. Growth is achieved through being broken to be made whole.[43]

This imagery is also reflected in mythology through the hero's descent into the underworld. Common throughout ancient mythology as well as modern stories, is the hero venturing into the underworld to confront the darkness within, emerging stronger and more whole than before they entered. Examples of the underworld include the literal underworld from mythology, a place of the dead, or a subterranean space or cave. The underworld is also thought of as the domain of the unconscious. Venturing into the unconscious exposes us to the demons and darkness lurking within our mind. The underworld is a place of danger, death, and confrontation with the enemy. It is through this confrontation with danger that the hero is able to grow, causing the underworld to be a place of transformation, rebirth, and growth. Returning from the underworld is comparable to a resurrection as the hero ascends from the land of death back to the surface world of life, often gaining something valuable from their pursuit. Growth and improvement are achieved through descending into the underworld, facing the danger within, and returning to the surface with something gained from the experience.

But no one said growth was easy. Growth is not easy. In fact, growth can often be difficult and painful. But growth can be achieved. A metal sword is forged in a scathing fire. A diamond is formed from intense heat and pressure.

However difficult this process is, the result justifies itself. Although uncomfortable, growth is attainable to all those who pursue it.

We should want growth. We should want to become more than what we are. And to grow, we should welcome the pain that comes with this pursuit.

Death of the Individual: Our Modern Machine

There are no more individuals. That singular and independent form of Being has been all but eliminated in our modern world. The individual person has been sacrificed to the machine of modernity, leaving only group members and pre-assigned roles to walk among us.

The individual is suffocated in this modern world we created. One must play the game to survive or fall between the cracks. Play the game of licenses, regulations, appointments, and approval. The modern world demands that everything come from this game. The food we eat must be regulated, the clothes we wear must be bought from a licensed source, and the content we consume must be approved for upload. Our modern machine must have it all.

To bypass this game we've created, with all its hoops and hurdles, would be a threat to the collective dream we have labored to build. Where there was once danger, our modern machine will regulate, investigate, and protect us until the only possible injury is suffocation under the complexity we've created. Food must be approved, says our modern machine. From the grocery store shelves, restaurant menus, and even the seeds you plant in your garden, they all must be approved by the modern machine. Barcodes, bureaucracies, appeals, and certifications. Everything must follow the rules of the game, or else it won't be allowed to play.

The collective dream for safety didn't stop with food, but expanded to movies, music, and video games. It all must be approved, or else it will not be allowed. The modern machine then comes for technology and innovation. Zoning, building codes, bylaws, and authorization. All acts of individual creation must be approved by the collective or else they will be stamped out. Then the modern machine comes for what an individual can read, say, or think. If the individual will not play with the modern machine, then it will turn against the individual.

The modern machine is soulless and removes the human spirit from all it touches. The game demands that entertainment become an industry. Farms become factories. People become employees who serve not just a boss, but a faceless corporation. The craftsman himself becomes a tool in a larger project where he has no autonomy, removed from his work and made into a pawn in a larger game. Communal politics become partisan as the party system dominates the individual. Everyone has a superior they serve and rules to follow. Even a transcendent experience of the Divine is codified into a rigid and dogmatic religious order where individuals must not step out of line. The wheels of the modern machine keep turning, grinding individuals into the collective.

Our cities and skylines were once an untapped wilderness full of danger and opportunity. After pioneers bring the wrath of nature under their control, communities grow, and the modern machine begins to emerge. Great countries are built by great individuals. But now the individual's hands are tied unless they act through the collective. Brave individuals once ventured forth to boldly go where no one has gone before. And surely, the modern machine will follow and swallow these individuals into the collective dream they unknowingly build.

Perhaps we should not dwell on our modern machine consuming all facets of life. Perhaps it's not even fair to call this modern machine "modern." Given enough time, simplicity becomes complexity, and people build complicated social systems. Eventually, these systems gain enough power to smother the individual entirely. This happened to the ancient Egyptians, Romans, and Chinese. Many kingdoms have fallen under the weight of their own complexity. Perhaps this is a tale as old as time. But the question still remains, what must be done about the loss of individualism at the hands of our modern machine? What do we individuals do when it feels as if the individual is powerless?

The answer is not to become angry at the machine. The machine is perpetuated by the fearful who desire safety and control above all else. And let them have it, for feelings of safety and the illusion of control is all they will ever have. They will not create as the individual can. They will not thrive on their own as the individual does. They are the collective, and until they become individuals, they will remain a part of the modern machine. The modern machine is inevitable as a protection for the weak.

There are two paths for the individual when confronting the modern machine. The first path is that of the Shepherd, whose goal is to maintain the health of the modern machine and guard against possible corruption. Entropy exists in all parts of life. Things are always falling apart and need to be maintained. The modern machine is inevitable and so is its decay. Good and virtuous individuals are needed to keep the modern machine in check and ensure the machine is aimed at creating Goodness for the community. Although it may be frustrating and exhausting, there is great honour in maintaining the health of our modern machine.

The second path is that of the Pioneer, who searches for where the modern machine has not touched, and begins to build there. It's not cold and calculated regulation that leads to human flourishing. Prosperity is created by individuals, not their societies. If an individual *must* be an individual and feels suffocated by the modern machine of their society, then this is an opportunity for exploration, adventure, and ultimately, the creation of a shining light to illuminate the darkness.

Part II
The Collective

Be Wary of Ideology

When the ambiguity of life can cause you grief,
Close your mind and don't question belief.
No questions, no confusion.
Only answers and the solution.
They're seductive, simple, and seemingly airtight.
Choose an ideology to make the world right.

But you know what they say, if it's too good to be true, then it probably is. If your worldview is unable to consider that your perspective might be wrong, then you could be suffering from an ideology.

The term "ideology" comes from two Greek words meaning "patterned reasoning."[44] Patterned reasoning is essentially what an ideology is, especially relating to political, moral, or economic thinking. To say you subscribe to an ideology is to imply you use that pattern of reasoning to approach problems. Liberals will approach the world from a liberal perspective, conservatives will be generally more conservative in their thinking, and so on.

Ideologies offer a way to perceive the world and our place in it. They often seem reasonable, and even intuitive. However, they lack nuance. They're unable to see shades of gray. When an ideology takes hold of one's mind, their perception and thinking are tainted, and they become extreme in their consideration.

If only the world were as simple as an ideology proclaims. The world is anything but simple. And any worldview that denies the complexity and uncertainty of reality does a disservice to the pursuit of truth.

If truth is our goal, then ideologies are dangerous. They're appealing and valuable, but often incomplete. They have a fatal flaw they just can't defeat.

Ideologies are rigid and aren't open to the possibility of their miscalculations. Ideologues, and all those who are possessed by an ideology, perceive the world through a particular lens that isn't necessarily accurate. They force the world to fit a predefined framework, even when the truth of reality differs from their ideological beliefs.

An ideology is a parasite of the mind. It makes its victim incapable of thinking beyond the scope of its prescribed worldview. An ideology sets the parameters of how to think, even if reality differs from the conclusions of the ideology. Almost always, reality isn't as simple as an ideology suggests.

Ideology hates nuance.

An ideology is fixed, rigid, and dead. There's no life to an ideology except for the initial euphoria of feeling enlightened. What follows is a cold and clinging existence to a worldview one must defend at all costs. One's sanity and psychological wellbeing depend on it.

There can be no reasoning with ideologues. They're close-minded to alternative views and will cling to their ideology out of fear of the unknown. When questioned, they seem confident. When shown possible errors in their ideology, they become defensive and angry—as if someone were deflating their raft and they fear falling into the raging ocean below them. They will cling to their raft at all costs to avoid the confusion and chaos of uncertainty.

To be fair, ideologies are based on truth, but only a half-truth. Socialists correctly identify the dangers of greed, profit through exploitation, and the corrupt tendencies of the wealthy. However, they fail to recognize the merits of charity, private donations, and community altruism. Capitalists embrace the efficiency of free markets to produce wealth and prosperity, while they ignore those who fall between the cracks, and neglect the reality of wealth allowing for corruption and unequal power over the political process. Libertarians correctly point out the dangers of authoritarian rule and the harm that comes from tyranny, but they neglect the harm caused by the absence of authority. Authoritarians understand the necessity for stability and control, but suffocate the human spirit and are prone to abuses of power. Religious believers recognize the importance of our relationship with the Divine and Transcendent, while atheists often point out the dangers and harm of rigid religious extremism. Ideologies are grown from a kernel of truth but become corrupted and deformed as they move away from their seeds. Ideologies become mere shadows and illusions of the world's complexity.

Be suspicious of those who have all the solutions yet ask no questions. An ideology can have no blind spots and leave no room for uncertainty. Listen to those who admit their ignorance, for they're not trying to convince themselves of what they do not know.

The light of truth can be blinding. But it is better to have seen truth and be unable to articulate its form than to falsely present truth without the nuance it deserves. Claiming truth without nuance is to neglect the richness of the world. Whereas the world is complicated and always changing, an ideology rigidly puts reality into a box and says, "This is it."

Reality cannot be put into a box, since the box of our comprehension cannot contain the vastness of reality. This would imply that our comprehension is beyond reality, able to fully encapsulate reality. However, reality will always be one step ahead of those who try to perceive it.

But there are those among us who believe they've solved the riddle of life and offer you a box. I warn you from taking this box. This box will rob you of truth and make you a slave to a system you will feel compelled to defend. You will be forced to bend the world to fit into your box, and when your box is threatened, you will be shaken to your core and guard it with your life.

To submit yourself to an ideology is to put yourself in a box, lock up your mind, and throw away the key. Refuse being boxed in by an ideology. When you put the world into a box, you box yourself in as well. You no longer see the truth unless it's through the lens of your ideology. When committed to an ideology, the world you see is that of shadows of their true form, distorted by your certainty.

To think for oneself isn't as convenient as being absorbed into an ideological worldview. Although it isn't an easy path, thinking independently, free from the restrictions of an ideological parasite, is a more fruitful path to truth and prosperity.

If we are to resist the seductive sway of an ideology, we must embrace the unknown and be comfortable with uncertainty. Above all else, an ideology provides certainty and feelings of safety. When one's ideology is challenged, our fundamental need for safety is threatened. When confronted with ideas contrary to our ideology or worldview, the human brain struggles to remain calm. Instead, the brain's capacity for critical thinking, understanding, and rationality are replaced by our fight-or-flight response. When one is under the influence of an ideology, challenges to their ideological worldview are perceived as a physical threat.[45] This is no way to pursue truth. Challenges to our worldview are not a threat, but are instead an opportunity for correction and aligning oneself with truth, even if our new conclusions differ from our initial ideological starting point.

The solution to one ideology is not another ideology, nor ignoring all ideologies. The solution to ideologies is resisting the fear of the unknown and being comfortable perceiving the world with nuance and complexity.

Or perhaps we don't fear the unknown, rather, we fear not knowing. To believe something inaccurately highlights one's ability to be deceived or think wrongly. Perhaps our fear is in realizing that we are not who we thought we were. We are human beings with minds prone to error. We are capable of making mistakes, being lied to, and being fooled. We often have faults in our judgment and believe things that are false. This can be a difficult truth to accept for those who think they are incapable of being incorrect. We must realize that being wrong is okay, and that being wrong is a necessary step toward being right. Perhaps we won't ever know some things with certainty, and we'll be okay even if we don't know.

Embracing the unknown as an opportunity to learn is liberating and allows us to become closer to the truth. Only through resisting the fear of not knowing and withstanding the pull of ideological thinking, can we perceive the world as it truly is—not as a world of black and white, but of beautiful shades of gray.

The Value of Truth

Truth.

What is truth?

Truth is how things really are. Truth is the world independent of your bias or opinion. Truth is the ultimate bedrock on which all things are based.

Truth does not change. Truth is the anchor of reality and grounds for existence. Truth is what is real. Truth is reality how it is. The opposite of truth is falseness. The opposite of truth is what reality is not. Falsehoods and lies misrepresent reality. They paint reality in a manner that it is not.

You may ask, "So what? What good is truth when I can speak falsely? Can I not bend the world to my will? Isn't reality able to change for me? And even if reality does not change, why not speak of reality however I wish?"

For your own good and for the sake of everyone else, I urge you to align yourself with the truth. Not because lying is wrong, but because there is a benefit through the truth.

Truth is how things are. Truth is sewn into the fabric of reality. Truth *is* reality. Why would you want to stand against reality? Why would you want to deprive yourself or others of how things are? They say, "The truth will set you free." Free from what? Free from confusion, delusion, and how things are not. It is through truth that we better understand the world and can better our lives.

Truth is the soil from which good things grow. Truth is the stable foundation on which thigs can be built. Try building a structure with inaccurate measurements. Try laying brick on falsehoods and fiction. Foundations built on falsehoods and inaccuracies are like sand beneath a tower. The tower will crumble unless it's built on something solid. Truth is the solid foundation on which we should build. Dare I say, truth is the only foundation that can be built on with stability. Anything built on falsehood will eventually collapse and crumble beneath its own inaccuracy. There's a reason why the truth is sometimes referred to as "the light." Because without the light of truth, we walk in darkness.

There is value in aligning yourself with what is real over what is false. What good is it to believe a lie over truth? What good is it to view this world with glasses that distort your vision? To deny truth, or to ignore it, is to exist in opposition to reality. Why would one want to stand against reality? Why deny the truth that reality is built on? Surely this is foolish and does no good. Willingly denying the truth is to cover your eyes with a blindfold and stumble over obstacles you could have avoided had you seen reality for how it is. To move without stumbling, or best avoid stumbling, we must see the path before us. We must align with truth and regard truth and accuracy as the basis for all that is real.

Why would we want to perpetuate lies? Why intentionally misrepresent the truth? Why intentionally spread what is not real? If falsehood and inaccuracy cause us to stumble, what does it do for others? Why would we spread ripples of deceit throughout our social circles? Why would we want to live in a world where everyone around us stumbles? The way you speak of the world informs the worldview of others. Spreading lies only causes those around you to think of the world inaccurately. To lie is to give out blindfolds to others. To lie is to taint our shared spaces with inaccuracy. You think you're an island, but you're really on a boat with others. If you fail to give proper directions, the likelihood our shared boat will crash and sink increases dramatically.

What is the antidote to sinking our shared vessel? We must align with the truth. We must align ourselves with how reality is. Even when the truth may be uncomfortable, it is valuable. Even when the truth is hard, in its firmness is a love that is beneficial.

The universe functions according to laws and rules. The key to the Good Life is to live in accordance with the rules of reality. What good is it to deceive ourselves about how the world works? What benefit is there in not understanding the workings of this universe?

In this universe, governed by its laws, there are conditions for both poverty and prosperity. Why would you ignore how each is created? Why would you ignore the inputs that create the outputs? Surely you want the outputs, but you don't look for the inputs. And some of us see the inputs and deny their relation to the outputs, expecting reality to work out in our favor when we try to swim against its raging current. If we don't want to drown as the current moves us, we must understand how the current functions. Understanding the truth of the current is valuable if you want to swim. Sink or swim, the choice is yours.

To oppose these cosmic laws is to oppose truth itself. And just as an input will cause an output, disobeying the cosmic laws will earn cosmic punishment. Breaking human laws is one thing, but challenging the laws of nature? This is another matter entirely. As beings constrained by nature, this is a higher authority we cannot defy. Roman statesman, Marcus Tullius Cicero, speaks to the cosmic laws and warns of going against nature.

> *"And there will not be different laws at Rome and at Athens, or different laws now and in the future, but one eternal and unchangeable law will be valid for all nations and all times, and there will be one master and ruler, that is, God, over us all, for he is the author of this law, its promulgator, and its enforcing judge. Whoever is disobedient is fleeing from himself and denying his human nature, and by reason of this very fact he will suffer the worst penalties, even if he escapes what is commonly considered punishment."*[46]

For those who have a watered-down understanding of God, imagine God as the underlying laws of nature. To go against nature is to suffer the consequences of nature and the cosmic order. To align with the cosmic order is to reap the benefits of nature's laws.

This is similar to the Buddhist idea of rebirth and Karma, or the notion "what goes around comes around." As a general rule, what you put out into the world comes back to you. If you do good, then good will happen to you. If you do bad, then bad will happen to you. Although some critics say that Karma is a hokey pokey belief in supernatural forces, it seems based in practicality. For example, if you're an asshole, then odds are that people will treat you with coldness and cruelty. Alternatively, if you treat people with kindness and love, they're more likely to treat you in a similar manner. If you go to a job and work hard, do well, and strive for the best, then you'll get more rewards and opportunities. If you're kind to others, you'll be more likely to build relationships with good people, which in turn offers you more of the good things of life. If you have healthy habits, you'll likely be a healthy person. With the exceptions of randomness and tragedy, life unfolds according to our participation in the laws of nature. Our life unfolds in our relation to truth.

Why would we want to oppose truth? Why would we want to resist reality? Psychologist and cultural commentator, Jordan Peterson, spoke about one's opposition to truth and the effects it can have on one's life. He says:

"I have never, in all my years as a clinical psychologist, and this is something that really does terrify me, I have never seen anyone ever get away with anything at all, even once... Well, maybe you disagree. Maybe you think that people get away with things all the time. I tell you, I've never seen it. What I see instead is that a thing happens, right? Someone twists the fabric of reality. And they do it successfully because it doesn't snap back at them at that moment.

And then like two years later, something unravels, and they get walloped and they think, "Oh my God, that's so unfair." And then we track it, and we ask, "what happened before that?" "This." "Well, then what?" "This." "And then what?" "This." "And then what?" "Oh, this. Oh that's where it went wrong." Yeah, because you can't twist the fabric of reality without having it snap back. It doesn't work that way, and why would it, because what are you going to do? Twist the fabric of reality? I don't think so."[47]

We ultimately can't cheat the truth. We can't change the fabric of reality. We are not bigger than truth. Truth exists beyond us. And if we want a prosperous life, then we must prosper according to the rules of reality. To live a valuable life, we must align with the ultimate value. To live well, we must live in truth.

Value Itself

What we should strive for isn't a commitment to an ideological aim, but for whatever promotes goodness and human flourishing.

We must aim past the rigid values of narrow thinking and pursue the core of value itself. The question isn't what values we should have. The question is, what is it about values that make them valuable? Isolate this factor and aim at this instead. This is Value itself—the thing at the heart of all shared religious and ideological seduction. It is the kernel of truth without the dogmatic leach hanging off its side, sucking out its elixir.

But the problem with this truth is that it's always just one step ahead of us. It's transcendent, beyond our world. While we can clearly see values, we only get mere glimpses into the nature of Value itself.

The World on Our Shoulders

Figure 4: Statue of Atlas in Rockefeller Center, New York City. Changed to black-and-white.

What Does Atlas Hold On His Shoulders?

In Rockefeller Center of New York City, a two-tonne statue of the Titan god, Atlas, is depicted with a globe on his shoulders as he struggles beneath its weight. After leading the Titans in their war against Zeus and the Olympians, Atlas faced a unique punishment. While the other Titans were cast into Tartarus, similar to Hell for the ancient Greeks, Zeus chose a fitting punishment for Atlas—one he would endure for eternity. Atlas was imprisoned where the Heavens met the Earth and was condemned to hold up the sky, to hold on his shoulders the overwhelming might of the Heavens from crashing down onto the Earth. In other words, Atlas was punished by the gods to hold up the world.

Other versions of the story depict Atlas holding up a globe or carrying the weight of the world on his shoulders. Whether Atlas carries the Heavens or the Earth on his shoulders, the effect is the same. Dropping his burden would either be the collapse of the Earth or the collapse of Heavens, causing the sky to come crashing down onto the Earth. Whether Atlas carries the sky or the globe, he carries the fate of the world on his shoulders.

But why is Atlas punished by carrying the fate of the world? Perhaps this punishment wasn't just for opposing the gods in the Titanomachy, the ten-year war between the Titans and the Olympians, but perhaps his punishment was for taking the initiative to lead the Titans in battle. Perhaps this tale from ancient Greece is to suggest that leaders are condemned to carry the fate of the world on their shoulders.

It's interesting to consider our effects on the world around us. It's not just leaders who have influence over the world. Each individual has the capacity to affect their family, friends, and communities. Human beings exist in networks. We are embedded in an interconnected system of relationships with one another.

A sociological idea claims at most six social connections separate every person in the world. For example, your co-worker's, friend's, cousin's, roommate are separated from you by only four degrees. The idea is that every human being on Earth is separated from you by no more than six degrees. There's a website called "The Oracle of Bacon"[48] or the "The Six Degrees of Kevin Bacon" which demonstrates this sociological phenomenon in action by showing how every person in the film industry is separated by no more than six degrees from the actor Kevin Bacon. The same rule holds true for every person around the world and seems to confirm the old adage that, "No man is an island entire to itself."[49]

Individuals have tremendous power to influence the world. If we try to visualize the social web of human beings, we soon discover we are closer to one another than previously thought. Our interactions with one another influence the social world around us causing ripple effects far beyond what our eyes can see. What we put out into the world through our actions, attitudes, and effects on others can reach thousands of people. And those thousands of people will go on to influence millions of people, allowing our influence to spread throughout the globe.

It's not just leaders like Atlas who are condemned to hold the world on their shoulders. Each individual person has the capacity to influence the world around them, holding the world on their shoulders as well.

Whereas some regard this condemnation of shouldering the world as a punishment from the gods, it's more accurately a metaphor for the inevitable influence we hold over our community. Atlas is us. We are condemned by the gods to hold up the world. The responsibility for your community rests on your shoulders. Whether you like it or not, your actions will have an inevitable ripple effect on everyone you encounter. Your actions matter.

Some have said that Atlas should simply shrug. Ayn Rand and her Objectivist philosophy[50] proposes that rather than bearing the weight of the world on our shoulders, we should shrug and let the world fall. After all, cynics may argue that we are under no obligation to hold up the world. The fate of Atlas is that of a slave, condemned to suffer a punishment against his voluntary will. We are not slaves and should throw off a burden of this tyrannical nature, some might say.

While our liberation sounds appealing, it's wishful thinking. For Atlas to refuse his fate and shrug the world from his shoulders, the sky would come crashing down upon him, bringing chaos and destruction. As human beings, we face the same punishment as Atlas—and the same consequence for shrugging the world from our shoulders.

When we say one holds up the world, what does this mean? What is the world being held up from? Whether we recognize it or not, every individual has the ability to uphold goodness in the world. Each individual has the capacity to hold up the world towards the highest ideal and to strive against all hardships to prevent the world from falling. We all play a role in preventing the flame of goodness from being extinguished.

But what's the harm in the world falling? What happens when someone drops their responsibility to the world's wellbeing from their shoulders? What would happen if Atlas were to drop the world? What is the world being held up from? From dark times. From trouble and suffering. From chaos and conflict. From oppression and injustice. From the fall of humanity from the garden of paradise. And the world falls when enough people refuse to carry the success of the world. The success of the world is dependent on our participation in the pursuit of goodness.

Of course, Atlas can shrug and reject his responsibility to uphold the wellbeing of the world. But to shrug and give up would be foolish since the world on his shoulders is the same world on which he stands. If Atlas lets the world fall, then he will fall as well. One is not forcefully obligated to care for their neighbor or pursue the common good, but it is in our best interest to do so. We aren't legally required to carry the world on our shoulders, but our refusal to take personal responsibility for the wellbeing of the world is akin to letting it fall. If you won't hold up the world, then who will?

Jean-Paul Sartre famously said, "Man is condemned to be free."[51] What is more, man is condemned to live with the consequences of our freedom. Not just the consequences for ourselves, but for the communities in which we live. We can either view this condemnation as a punishment from the gods to suffer the horrors of this world, or as an opportunity for each of us to do our part to tilt our communities toward Goodness the light of the Transcendent.

And thus, the fate of the world rests on your shoulders. Now go and hold it high, as a beacon for all to see.

Tolkien, Gandalf, and Wisdom in Times of Hardship

Tragedy is as old as the human species. Whether it be a natural disaster, war, government corruption, or a pandemic, hard times fall upon us. It's easy to get scared or angry when the shadow of darkness looms overhead. It's easy to become one with the darkness and let our worst impulses possess us when faced with tragic circumstances. But this isn't how things have to be.

Times of hardship can be devastating. To be honest, I sometimes find myself getting angry and ready to give up in the most challenging circumstances. I know I'm not the only one who finds peace and composure to be difficult during times of hardship. I know I'm not the only one who's tempted to give in or lash out. It's in these moments that I'm reminded of a scene from *The Lord of the Rings*. In times of struggle, I feel like we're Frodo, carrying a stress that feels unbearable. And like Frodo, we whine and protest, "I wish it need not have happened in my time."

Gandalf, a mentor and friend of Frodo responds, "So do all who live to see such times, but that is not for them to decide. All we have to decide is what to do with the time that is given to us."[52]

It seems that the idea expressed by Tolkien is that of resilience in the face of adversity. This is a timeless idea that gives rise to prosperity. In fact, it is the only path that can give rise to human flourishing in response to tragedy and suffering. And even if your triumph is unsuccessful, what better alternative do you have than to accept your circumstances and face life's hardships heroically and courageously?

Has something happened that ruined your life? Did tragedy strike and rain down unbearable suffering? If you're a human being, odds are this has happened to you at some point. Has the government or corporations done something stupid to make things worse? Yup, welcome to politics. Tragedy and incompetence are the stories of human history. So, what are you going to do about it? Are you going to whine that you wish the current problem wasn't happening? I'm sure that helped the people living during the Bubonic plague. Are you going to complain about the government and wish that if only they did something different then things would be better? That's an original thought. I'm sure that whining helped the soldiers who literally fought Nazis, a group that was committed to genociding the Earth for the perfect Aryan race. Yeah, I'm sure they wished that Nazis weren't a thing either. I bet they really complained about it when they were storming the beaches of Normandy under machine-gun fire, many knowing they would never see their families again. So keep going, tell me how you wish this thing had never happened.

No one living in times of tragedy wished for their suffering. But we don't get to choose what time we're born in, nor do we blow the winds of fate. It's not helpful to complain and wish this thing hadn't happened. The important thing to ask is how you're going to respond to these circumstances. How are you going to make the best out of it? It has been said, "We can't change the wind, but we can adjust our sails."[53]

Your God or government won't magically make things better. But you can. We all share a responsibility in keeping our society together as we hobble from tragedy to tragedy (and we've been doing this for a very long time).

Another insight from Gandalf;

> *"Some believe that it is only great power that can hold evil in check, but that is not what I have found. I found it is the small everyday deeds of ordinary folk that keep the darkness at bay. Small acts of kindness and love."*[54]

We are the ones who keep the darkness at bay. We are the ones who can spread either good or bad into the world. No tragedy is large enough to rob us of our choice in how we respond to life's circumstances.

So, let's just keep focusing on the important things, like our family, friends, and community, genuine human connections and our relationships with others. Perhaps some hobbies or activities you've been trying and shows you're watching. Maybe a book you're reading or something you're excited to do over the next few weeks. Something you want to learn or get better at. Things will eventually work themselves out and life will get better.

We don't choose what happens to us, but we can choose the people we become in spite of our circumstances.

The Stories We Share: Creation From Chaos

Chaos is a condition that plagues the human psyche. There's something about chaos and disorder that people dislike. Unfortunately for these folks, human history is riddled with confusion, mayhem, and destruction. In other words, chaos is constant.

We're no stranger to chaos. As the world emerges from the worst global pandemic in nearly a century, we confront an economic and mental health crisis. If that wasn't bad enough, Russia invaded Ukraine, Taiwan fears they're next, and global temperatures are rising, spawning unprecedented environmental disasters. It seems the world is a very chaotic place indeed.

But luckily for us, chaos isn't something to be feared. In fact, the oldest stories of our species suggest that chaos is a necessary force for creation. This is important to us because chaos, and all the destruction and suffering that comes with it, seem to be a constant reality of our world. But we must remember that it is from this chaos that things emerge. For us to act, there must first be chaos.

Mythology and ancient stories across human cultures represent chaos as a necessary force for creation. The necessity of chaos is an idea at the core of humanity, represented in the creation myths of ancient Greece, ancient Mesopotamia, and the ancient Hebrew peoples, along with the creation myths of the Indigenous Haudenosaunee and Aztec peoples. Human mythology suggests that chaos is *essential* to the world, with chaos as the necessary condition for creation.

First up, ancient Greek mythology speaks of a world before anything, and this world was pure chaos. Interestingly, the Greeks thought this chaos necessarily produces Gaia, the divine spirit of the Earth, fertility, and mother of all life.

This notion of creation coming from chaos is also present in the ancient Mesopotamian myth of the Enuma Elish. This tale speaks of a hero-god, Marduk, who battles the goddess of primordial chaos, Tiamat. Marduk defeats the chaotic goddess and physically creates the world from her pieces.

Biblical mythology shares a similar idea of chaos and creation. In the opening lines of Genesis, the world is said to be a chaotic and formless void from which God then creates the order of our universe.

Indigenous mythology of the Haudenosaunee (Iroquois) peoples also speaks of creation coming from chaotic circumstances. The Haudenosaunee creation story speaks of a woman falling from the Sky Islands. After falling into the chaotic oceans of the Earth and nearly drowning, several animals help the Sky Woman safely onto the back of the Turtle where the land of our world was grown from.

This conception of creation arising from chaos is also represented in the Aztec mythology of the Mexica peoples. From the void and chaos of nothingness came Ōmeteōtl, the supreme God and creator of the universe.

Out of disorder and chaos comes a force for good. These stories all speak of creation coming from chaos, and chaos as a necessity for creation and all the good things of this world.

Through ancient stories and cross-cultural mythology, we learn that chaos is not only a destructive force to be feared, but a condition for creation and goodness. These stories resonate with all cultures because they remind the human being of their sacred purpose when encountering the trials and tribulations of this world.

Ultimately, understanding the human being as a force for creation when encountering chaos is a common theme shared across all human cultures.

These are the stories that define us as human beings. These are the stories that move cultures and create religions. Civilizations are founded on these stories and their mythologies become an eternal testament to the prosperity of the human spirit. This is what's at the heart of the arts, and the beautiful end of literature, film, and the humanities. This is what stories are at their core, and these are the stories we share.

Problems and Potential

Problems and potential. That's all there is.

That's what's out there in the world. There are problems, and there's the potential for problems to be solved. Problems are very obvious. Suffering, poverty, inefficiency, injustice, tyranny, evil, and apathy plague every human society. Problems are undeniable. We see them everywhere. But with these problems comes the potential for them to be alleviated. Suffering is an opportunity to illuminate the darkness.

This is the story of humanity. These are the best stories we tell ourselves. This is the core of all mythology and the foundation for every great civilization. Within problems lies the potential for them to be solved. And this is what human beings do. We solve problems and make life better.

When faced with starvation, humanity learned to forage and farm. When faced with predators, humanity hunted our threats like prey. When faced with enemies, humanity became warriors. When faced with disease, humanity became doctors. When separated by the raging oceans of Earth, humanity built ships to carry us across the waters. When our cities lacked water and the ability to sustain life, humanity constructed sprawling aqueducts and plumbing systems to bring water to our people. When faced with darkness, humanity created light. Humanity has evolved to overcome problems. We have evolved to see problems, and we thrive by working towards their solution.

We must remember that there will always be problems. When one problem is solved, the human mind finds another. And when there are no problems left, the human mind will invent them out of its compulsive need for adversity. Problems are sewn into the fabric of reality.

This idea is brilliantly represented in the mythology of Tolkien, author of *The Lord of The Rings*. Prior to the events of his most famous series, Tolkien's work, *The Silmarilion*, accounts for the creation of the world and the nature of reality. In this account, problems are fundamental to reality. *The Discord of Melkor* tells a story of how problems and discord entered the world.

In short, Eru, or the One (God), created the Many. These were the Ainur and were the "offspring of his thought." The Ainur are essential to the nature of reality. They all sang the Divine music in beautiful harmony. All of creation sang together. Until Melkor, one of the Ainur, decided to take for himself more power and glory through his contribution and broke the harmony. Through the discord of Melkor, the harmony was shattered, and the cosmic music fell out of tune. The world used to be in harmony, and then it was broken.[55]

This creation story seems to suggest the notion that consciousness seeks harmony and strives to return to this time before the discord. Discord is the problem, and it is fundamental to reality. There will always be discord. But in this discord is the potential for harmony. Problems can be solved and harmony can be pursued. Though we must recognize that we can never attain total harmony with the universe. The discord of Melkor is sewn into the fabric of reality and the world will always appear to us as problems to be solved. The world will always appear to us as music out of tune. But it is through striving for the good that we become part of the world's harmony.

A similar idea is expressed in the Biblical myth of the Tower of Babel.

The Tower of Babel

Now the whole world had one language and a common speech. As people moved eastward, they found a plain in Shinar and settled there.

They said to each other, "Come, let's make bricks and bake them thoroughly." They used brick instead of stone, and tar for mortar. Then they said, "Come, let us build ourselves a city, with a tower that reaches to the heavens, so that we may make a name for ourselves; otherwise we will be scattered over the face of the whole earth."

But the LORD came down to see the city and the tower the people were building. The LORD said, "If as one people speaking the same language they have begun to do this, then nothing they plan to do will be impossible for them. Come, let us go down and confuse their language so they will not understand each other."

So the LORD scattered them from there over all the earth, and they stopped building the city. That is why it was called Babel—because there the LORD confused the language of the whole world. From there the LORD scattered them over the face of the whole earth.

(Genesis 11, 1-9)

It seems this story is describing the nature of reality and the patterns of human civilization. At first, everyone is on the same page. We have shared values and shared goals. We decide to build a tower to God, also thought of as the highest ideal and the ultimate pursuit. Over time, things fall apart. Problems emerge. Where there are people, soon there will be drama. Conflicts emerge. Disagreements arise. People fight. Those who started with shared values eventually fracture into warring camps of opposing values. People have different goals and see the world in different ways. Metaphorically speaking, people speak different languages and can no longer understand one another. The shared tower to God becomes abandoned.

This is human civilization. This is the story of history. Our task for the future is to bring people together, understand one another, return to a state of harmony, and continue building the tower to God.

There will always be problems to be solved. There will always be the discord of Melkor. People will always fracture and begin speaking different languages, both literally and metaphorically. Even though problems will always be present, the meaning of life comes from striving to solve these problems and making life better.

Those Who Build and Those Who Destroy

There are those among us who are driven by anger and destruction. They are hyper-critical, resentful, and quick to spot the errors of the world. We all know these people. These angry critics. Those who wish for your joy to become ashes in your mouth. Quick to criticize, slow to praise, and only praise when it serves a deeper criticism.

You're excited about your new phone? But the buzzkill is quick to mention the slave labour of its production. You're enjoying the holiday season? The buzzkill will always remind you of the genocidal and colonialist roots you celebrate. You're optimistic about the future and excited about an opportunity? The buzzkill will criticize your excitement. The buzzkill will hold your happiness against you so long as you are not as outraged as they are.

The cosmic buzzkills are those who feel the need to dampen the spirits of all those around them. There can be no happy moment around these critics, for they are quick to remind others that even perceived good things are built on bloody foundations.

And building? They do no such thing. They criticize that which has been built without building themselves. For them, their goal is to destroy and tear down that which has been built, without offering a building for the future. They seek to tear down, rather than build up. They serve only destruction, these cosmic buzzkills.

They claim to be outraged on behalf of the oppressed, while their spirit is cold and ruthless. They condemn the slaver, while they smile when handed a whip. They say the aim of their criticism is for a higher good. But when the time comes, they would rather talk than walk.

And it is for this reason that we should not worry about these comic buzzkills—they don't *do* anything. They don't build. They don't plant. They don't create. That which prospers cannot be built by forces of destruction.

Nothing can be built on the foundation of destruction. Anger and resentment are not self-sustaining and will always crumble. These destroyers will never prosper.

These servants of destruction can only destroy. Although they walk possessed by anger, these servants of destruction will always walk among us. But they will not build a new world. They will only destroy the old world and perish among its ruins. They die and fade into obscurity, left behind as the new world is created.

But you, my friend, do not have to worry about these servants of destruction. For you build while they destroy. For you plant while they point fingers. For you create while they condemn. Nothing will grow from their cold and empty hearts. But your heart will create. Your soul will build to new heights.

Good things planted are enjoyed by those who reap them. The trees you plant will provide shade for others. And that which you build will be a shelter against the suffering of the world. That which you create will be enjoyed by many, while the servants of destruction will bring joy to none.

Like up and down, and light and dark, the destroyers and creators go their separate ways. They to destroy, and you to create. Now go forth and build while aiming your sights at the highest good.

Rules For Argumentation: A Guide to Effective Communication

Throughout the years of our academic and work experience, my colleagues and I have discovered that effective communication is essential for productive dialogue, and productive dialogue is essential for mutual prosperity. Here are some guidelines to keep in mind when you find yourself in an argument.

1. Give your interlocutor's arguments the benefit of the doubt. Avoid strawmanning your interlocutor's argument by reducing it to something easier to refute. This is not productive, nor is it intellectually honest. Frame opposing arguments in their best possible light to properly engage with their contents.

2. To verify that you've correctly understood someone else's argument, try repeating it back to them. Rephrasing someone's argument in your own words and asking your interlocutor if this is an accurate description of their position is a great way to enhance understanding and avoid miscommunication.

3. Remember that although your interlocutor may be your opponent, they are not your enemy. Most of the time, they are a reasonable and well-intentioned person, just like you. Avoid ascribing immoral motivations to your interlocutor or attacking their character. These are not productive solutions to resolving the crux of the argument.

4. If you want to change the hearts and minds of those who disagree with you, then preserve your interlocutor's ego. Avoid attacking their character or making them feel stupid and inferior. This will only cause them to become defensive and less willing to participate in a fruitful discussion.

5. Set aside your ego by accepting uncertainty and confusion as your friend. In the famous words of Socrates, "All I know is that I know nothing." It's okay to be confused and have questions. Don't be afraid to ask questions for further clarity. Asking questions when you're confused shouldn't be

embarrassing and doesn't make you any less intelligent. Instead, it shows your humility, intelligence, and strength of character to admit your uncertainty.

6. To fully engage with your interlocutor, put yourself in their position and try to understand why a given conclusion makes sense to them. Avoid operating from an ideological and narrow-minded perspective.

Actually try to learn something from an argument rather than trying to prove your pre-existing conclusions. Socrates calls this uncomfortable state of unknowing, when we break through our previously held perspectives, "aporia," and says this is where true learning begins.[56] When we set aside our biases, we can experience a genuine philosophical discussion characterized by exploration, learning, and growth.

7. Last but not least, be kind and respectful. Your interlocutor is also a human being fighting their own battle of which you know nothing. Treat them like a friend and pay them a friend's respect.

The Problem with Politics

Politics is tribal, divisive, and fractures communities. Politics drives people apart rather than bringing people together. Politics is too much of a "team sport" while forgetting that we are all on the same team. Politics makes enemies out of scoring political points. Politics thrives on division.

Instead, we should recognize that different parties and political ideologies have the same aim. We all want what is best for our society. Aside from the bad apples bought off by corruption or plagued by negligence, people generally want what they think is best, regardless of party or political bias.

The founders of the American political system warned about the dangers of political parties. Before the birth of party politics, politicians operated as individuals who advocated for the needs of the people they represented. They were forced to communicate, cooperate, and work together to make laws. But once politicians align themselves with parties, the tribal nature of human beings takes over and politics becomes war.

If a political system creates the inability for average people to discuss it without anger and fury, then something has gone wrong. The problem with politics is that it is political. It's about division and separation over a unified pursuit of the common good. We should see each other as tackling the same problems from different angles. We should view each other as members of the same team, but with different positions. Like in sports, the defenders and the forwards have different styles of play, but they are both essential for a successful team. Both the left and the right have their flaws, but both wings of an airplane are needed to fly.

. . .

Broadly speaking, conservatives and members of the political right-wing are individualist, pragmatic, and often support traditional social institutions. Conservatives and right-wingers are often blind to the social and economic problems created by the institutions of our society, and tend to focus on individual choices and hard work as the path to success. Conservatives tend to blame individuals for their problems rather than problems with social systems.

Right-wingers are slower to recognize how social institutions and private businesses can become corrupt over time and bought off with money or other means of manipulation, causing members of society to fall between the cracks. Growing inequality seems inevitable and has been the case for all of human history until wars or other societal resets. Although society is stable, functional, and creates prosperity, it must also be maintained against corruption to function efficiently and prevent the unnecessary suffering of those at the bottom.

Conservatives generally oppose government funding to address social problems, and instead rely on private donations from individuals and communities since they believe government funding is either undeserved or inefficient at solving the problems they seek to address. Sometimes the solution of private funding is unreasonable for those who are alienated or live in a social network where community supports have collapsed.

Conservatives and right-wingers are often more traditional and are hesitant to support changes to social norms. Conservatives often view society as a complex mechanism and tend to focus on the unintended consequences and potential dangers of drastic social and economic change. Conservativism emphasizes the *conservation* of ideas and social institutions for pragmatic reasons and the inherent value of tradition. Conservatives see tradition as a tool that has functioned well enough to maintain order, stability, and keep society functioning without collapse.

...

In general, liberals and members of the political left-wing are collectivist, idealists, and guided by their ethical concerns for others, especially those who are oppressed. Liberals and left-wingers correctly point out the flaws in our social systems, particularly injustice, oppression, and inequality.

The political left acknowledges social and economic problems, and they believe they can actually solve these problems. The political left is often criticized for failing to provide workable and efficient solutions to the problems they try to solve. Oftentimes the solutions from political leftists are institutional in nature and focus on governmental interference, regulation, and oversight. These solutions are sometimes beneficial (such as regulating the banking system, displaying nutrition facts, ingredients, and caloric content on food products, posting speed limits, creating traffic laws, etc.) But sometimes the solution to solve one problem creates another. The creation of a government oversight department to solve one social problem often creates new problems of bureaucratic inefficiency, the concentration of power, and increased likelihood for governmental negligence or corruption, not to mention other unintended social or economic problems caused by the solutions to a previous problem. Leftists are quick to point out the corruption of for-profit enterprises while neglecting the corruption of the government institutions intended to solve social-economic problems.

Leftists are always searching for problems and define themselves by solving injustices in society. Leftists will define themselves in opposition to social-economic problems while they strive for a just society. If a problem is solved, leftists require new problems to solve or their identity collapses since they have nothing to strive against.

Leftists often neglect the productive and prosperous side of society, being too quick to dispose of our social institutions and 'tear things down' due to the oppression and inequality they may create. Rather than viewing society as something fragile and complex, the political left believes that problems can be solved with the right laws and actions taken by the government. The top-down solutions offered by leftists are often criticized as not working as anticipated and reducing the individual to a pawn of society without genuine agency or choice.

...

Solutions beginning with the individual seem more realistic for political prosperity than an institutional or systems-based approach. Individual corruption, vices, and moral failings are the reason for our societal problems. We cannot design society to remove the flaws of human nature since society is composed of human beings. Human society will reflect the qualities of human beings, both for better and for worse. Individual integrity and virtue are of fundamental importance to the success of society. Whether it be from the left or the right, corruption and incompetence collapse empires.

This is not to advocate for centrism. Centrism looks to find a balance between both sides and believes that political truth (if there is such a thing) lies in the middle, suggesting this is where the best policy is found. Radical centrism should also be avoided since a compromise is not always the best solution. Both the left and the right offer correct solutions to different problems, while sometimes a centrist middle ground is the best approach. Each issue must be evaluated separately without appealing to one's bias of 'team membership.' We must look past division to solve the problems we face and work together towards a better future.

Human social groups need a rallying point if they are to be united. Without a common cause, people become divided. In some sense, we need an enemy. So, what's the real enemy? Neglect, apathy, incompetence, and corruption. These vices go beyond party lines, and we must be diligent to prevent their triumph wherever they emerge.

When we strive for virtue, be at war with our vices, listen humbly, speak honestly, learn the limitations of our perspective, and hold the common good as the highest priority, this is when politics becomes productive.

The Path Forward: Neither Capitalism nor Socialism

Yes, it is true that capitalism has been the most efficient wealth-producing economic system in human history. Billions of people have been lifted out of poverty in large part to the global capitalist system, and most of our innovation in recent history is thanks to the capitalist incentive model.[57]

Also yes, capitalism creates massive inequality between the rich and the poor, and after enough time, will always create an ultra-wealthy elite that exists above the law and government.[58]

This is a problem, and some say socialism is the solution.

Yes, socialism with its wealth redistribution and increased government regulation can help reduce the gap between the rich and poor. Socialism is also effective at providing a social safety net for the poorest and most vulnerable members of society.

Also yes, socialism is inefficient at creating wealth, leading to economic stagnation and poverty after enough time. It's also concerning to look at the track record of socialist governments that become authoritarians who disregard human rights and freedoms while trampling on basic human dignity. Look no further than the history of Russia, China, Venezuela, Cuba, and North Korea, just to name a few.

So if both capitalism and socialism aren't the paths forward, then where do we go?

The solution is not the model we use, but the people acting within the model. A systems approach will never save humanity. A human is not a system, they are an individual guided by their will. And their will can aim either up or down in whichever system they inhabit.

Capitalism and socialism both suffer from the same fatal flaw—when the people with power lack virtue and neglect the common good, prosperity turns to ashes, and suffering becomes widespread. In the final analysis, the answer to the problem of government is neither politics nor economics, but rests in the individual character and virtue of human beings.

Powerful capitalists can use their wealth to lobby governments or bribe politicians. They can buy off public officials and take advantage of their employees. Capitalists can continue to hoard wealth and reinvest their profits for further gains, while taking from the poor and giving none of their wealth in return.

Powerful socialists can use their power to enrich themselves while neglecting the public good. The people put their faith in leaders to provide for them and look after their wellbeing, only to find that power corrupts, and their beloved leaders have ignored their oath of office. When power is put in the hands of a few, the many rely on the few to use their power responsibly. Socialist leaders and the workers of their administration are the same as you and me—susceptible to laziness, bad days, lack of motivation, and occasional incompetence.

On the other hand, socialists can withstand the temptation of corruption and use their power for the prosperity of the people. They can direct all their energy towards the common good and lead an administration of employees who do the same. In this situation, government funds are used efficiently, officials avoid corruption, and real solutions are implemented to increase the livelihood of the common citizen.

In the same vein, capitalists can produce the same prosperity for the people. Prior to the introduction of the Income Tax in the United States, most public libraries, museums, hospitals, infrastructure, and schools were funded and maintained by the wealthy elite. Those with power and wealth recognized their responsibility to give back to their community and actively work towards human flourishing. Capitalists can donate their wealth to charities and community organizations, they can pay their employees fairly, and can use their wealth to benefit humanity rather than themselves.

Ultimately, the good and bad directions of both capitalism and socialism rely on the character and virtue of human beings. It is impossible to create a system independent of humanity's flaws since these systems will be composed of human beings. Instead of debating socialism vs capitalism, let's focus our discussion on the importance of the character and virtue of a nation's leaders and citizens.

The Solution to Wealth Inequality & The Key to Maintaining Prosperity

What is profitable is not always what is best for long-term social stability. Personal profit must be used in service of the community's wellbeing or else the community will crumble.

Wealth collects at the top. Always has and always will. Royalty held most of the wealth in monarchies. Capitalists hold most of the wealth in democracies. Burial sites of hunter-gatherer and farming communities also indicate wealth inequality, with a minority of society possessing the majority of the wealth.[59] Even communist societies somehow result in a select minority of people owning most of the wealth and resources. Given enough time, the majority of wealth and resources always fall into the hands of a minority.

The unequal spread of wealth and resources is a fundamental problem for human communities. Not only do people get jealous of those who have more than them, but data from the World Bank shows that the more unequal a community's wealth is distributed, the more violent and unstable that community becomes.[60] The larger the divide between the rich and the poor, the more tension and conflict are created. People with the most wealth need to reinvest it into their communities and give much of it away or else history shows that their society will collapse into chaos.

Moreover, this is something that must be done voluntarily or else it doesn't work. You can't successfully end wealth inequality through taxation. If taxes are too high, wealthy people find legal ways to hide their wealth. And when the wealthy can't hide their wealth from taxation, then they just leave the country and take their wealth with them, causing none of their wealth to be taxed.

Throughout history, it's happened time and time again that when the rich become too rich and the poor become too poor, war and conflict erupt. You can even see this right now in the differences in crime rates between communities.

Communities with high wealth inequality have more violent crime than communities with less wealth inequality.[61]

Vast wealth inequality destabilizes social harmony. Eventually, when wealth inequality reaches a tipping point, war and revolution break out. This is what happened in the French Revolution, Russian Revolution, and Chinese Revolution(s), among countless other revolutions and social uprisings throughout history.

So what should be done about the problem of wealth inequality? Wealth inequality causes issues and eventually leads to social conflict. Wealth cannot be effectively redistributed through peaceful taxation. The alternative to peaceful taxation is a violent seizure of wealth, which is best to be avoided if a peaceful solution is desired. So what should be done about wealth inequality?

People with wealth need to voluntarily give much of their wealth away by reinvesting it back into their community. If not, their community will collapse. The key is that this choice must be voluntary. If the people with wealth do not want to voluntarily part with it, then the probability of a peaceful solution to the problems caused by wealth inequality is impossible.

Before the United States had an income tax, funding for schools, libraries, hospitals, and infrastructure was largely maintained by the voluntary contributions of the wealthy.[62] When Roman society was at its peak, infrastructure and public works were voluntarily paid for by wealthy senators.[63] Indigenous communities such as those in Western Canada would see the most successful chiefs accumulate the vast majority of wealth, which was then redistributed on a regular basis during the potlatch ceremony.[64] These historical instances suggest that for societies to survive and prosper, wealth must be voluntarily given away or reinvested into the community by the community's wealthiest members.

When the wealthiest members of our community refuse to voluntarily give away their wealth, the community degrades, and conditions worsen. History shows that unchecked wealth inequality leads to social collapse.

The mentality of profit as the ultimate goal is an ineffective long-term solution for a community. Profit motives can be hugely beneficial for countries, corporations, and communities, but the blessing turns into a curse when this profit is not voluntarily spread among the community.

Capitalism is not the problem. Greed and the refusal to give away wealth is the problem. Not just a moral problem, but a statistically verifiable social problem that leads to the collapse of civilizations and communities. The solution to wealth inequality is to give away wealth voluntarily and effectively to support what is needed for a community.

Governments do this to a mediocre degree of success after mismanagement, incompetence, and corruption are taken into account. What's better is when individuals and community organizations manage their own voluntary wealth redistribution. When wealth management is done properly at the community level, there's no need for a government to get involved.

We all have a responsibility to maintain the success of our communities, especially the wealthiest among us. Reinvesting wealth into the wellbeing of a community is the key to building and maintaining prosperity.

The Great Shadow

This world was created from the light of the Eternal Flame, from which the Great Shadow will necessarily follow. So long as humanity has stood on this world, illuminated by the Eternal Flame, the Great Shadow has been cast, taking on a life of its own. The Great Shadow will obscure and confuse, distorting the world within its grasp and possessing those lost within its darkness.

Most who have seen The Great Shadow are unable to recognize it, while those who can identify it are unable to speak of its form. Unable to be observed directly, The Great Shadow can be seen only through the darkness it casts. The Great Shadow is that which consumes and devours, possesses and paralyzes. What has been built can only be dismantled by shadow, and all that is built for destruction is guided by the seductive grasp of the darkness. Under the influence of the shadow, that which was flourishing becomes famine, and those who grow paradise stagnate in its decay. The evils of this world are generated by The Great Shadow, seeking to consume all into the void.

The armies of eternity have sought to wage war against The Great Shadow. With weapons drawn, they valiantly enter into the darkness guided by courage and conviction, with the shared intention of destroying The Great Shadow once and for all. Within the chaos and confusion of the darkness, the armies of eternity turn their blades on themselves, mistaking each other as agents of The Great Shadow and becoming locked in an eternal war.

The legions within the armies of eternity were once fixed on their shared enemy, but the darkness distorts their ranks, causing each other's banners to become sigils of The Great Shadow. Turning brother against brother, and sister against sister, the darkness blinds the noble warriors as they turn their blades on one another in the name of destroying The Great Shadow. Wherever The Great Shadow moves, the armies of eternity follow, forever dedicated to eradicating the darkness, forever condemned to be turned against one another.

Within The Great Shadow can be found an even greater light that can keep the darkness at bay. The Eternal Light can only be found by those who know how to find it and understand how to resist the possessing grasp of the darkness. This light is a small flame at first, but its blaze can be intentionally spread to overcome the darkness and drive The Great Shadow away, until one day it will return again with a newfound strength when the light has dimmed, and the story will continue.

Evil is Not the Problem

It's not those who do evil deeds that we should worry about. The real problem is those who would harm others in the name of the Good.

I was listening to a historical metal song about Walther Wenck, a Nazi general tasked by Hitler with defending Berlin at the end of World War II. The story fascinated me, so I read up on the intention behind the song. The historical account goes as follows:

> *"During the final battle of Berlin in 1945 the general of the 12th army, Walther Wenck realized that the end of the war was coming, and instead of trying to defeat the advancing Soviet forces as his orders were, he used his army to create an escape corridor out of Berlin for the civilians. For such an act he would surely have been sentenced to death, but instead he ended up being responsible for up to 250 000 people safely escaping the burning city of Berlin. For some this was a battle, for him this was a rescue operation."[65]*—
> Sabaton

This was a genuine act of heroism. Disobeying direct orders to save civilians under the threat of death is an astonishingly honourable act. However, it may be hard to reconcile this act of virtue with the fact that general Wenck was a Nazi.

Nazis are supposed to be evil. They're monsters. The world banded together to kill Nazis because their ideology was so horrendous. The inconvenient truth, however, is that Nazis believed they were justified in their beliefs. They sincerely thought they were building a better world in the name of goodness and prosperity. This should be the ultimate takeaway from Nazism and the Second World War—not that Nazis are bad, but that truly awful acts can be done by people who believe themselves to be good.

It's also hard to consider that it might not be entirely fair to characterize these regimes as evil.

What is 'evil'?

'Evil' isn't just 'bad' or 'super bad.'

'Evil' is to cause suffering *for the sake of suffering*.

Think of people who are evil and just want to cause suffering for the sake of suffering. School shooters, sadists, and those who torture animals... those sorts of people. Sure, evil people are a genuine threat on a local level or within communities; but fortunately, these people are not a threat on a global level. Evil isn't sustainable. Genuine evil can't get big enough to be a real threat in the same way an organization or government has influence over a large number of people.

A genuinely evil collective will always collapse in on itself before it becomes too big, if it can even form in the first place. This is because the type of people who are genuinely evil and enjoy causing suffering for the sake of suffering are usually unable to cooperate with others and are incapable of putting their own desires aside for a higher sense of good. It's no surprise that empires and governments usually collapse when they become too corrupt and disconnected from the Good. This is all to say that evil people aren't a substantial threat to humanity on a global level.

It's the awful people *who think they are good* and bring tremendous suffering to the world in keeping with their convictions who are the real problem. These were the Nazis, the Stalinists, and British Imperialism. If you could sit with (almost) any of these ideologues and ask why they're doing what they're doing, they will say it's the *right* and *good* thing for them to do. This is the real threat we have to watch out for. These beliefs can brainwash the minds of entire nations and bring people to commit unspeakable atrocities in the name of some warped and demented shadow of goodness.

Now it's time for some humility, to take a step back and recognize how far we're willing to go for our conception of goodness and to consider how our beliefs of justice may cause suffering and harm. Instead of labelling things we don't like as "evil," let's understand why these beliefs and ideologies are/were seductive and extract out of them what is genuine goodness, truth, and justice.

Because it's not the evil people we have to watch out for—it's good people like you who will do terrible things while convinced your actions are justified and morally pure.

Let Us Make Each Other's Friend

Come, friend, share your stories, and let us lose ourselves in the beauty of culture.

Let us be Prometheus and Athena rather than Romulus and Remus.

The experiences we have together will create a new world and new life. What will this life be? Will it be an empire born of murder? Or will our experience be a creative union aimed at the highest ideal?

Will our shared community be a colonial and exploitive people forged in the fires of conflict, destruction, and bloodshed? Will we be guided by the psychological force that destroys communities?

Or will we be a flourishing community? Rather than fighting, we could get along, get on the same page, and get our community together as an embodiment of the peaceful and prosperous potential that characterizes human civilization.

Will we pursue a good and virtuous life that can be whatever it decides to be? Will we aim at the life created by Prometheus and Athena? Will we aim at the life that was embodied in the people of Athens, both her history and myth? Or will we become Romulus and Remus, destined to forge an empire through blood and conquest?

We are not enemies, you and I. There is a friend and well-intentioned interlocutor within each of us. But, if there is a part of us that is enemies, let us have a discussion and demonstrate what Abraham Lincoln meant when he proclaimed, "I destroy my enemies when I make them my friends."[66] For he was a man who often strived to understand his adversary and truly know the contents of their heart. He was famous for saying, "I don't like that man. I must get to know him better."[67]

Of course, we will butt heads and disagree, but the ideal community is a tolerant and peaceful place for all people who wish to participate.

The community we create could be the best human civilization has to offer, or it could be the murder of Remus and the foundation of an empire.

What will this community be?

Statues to Virtue and Vice

What is a good person? Is there such a thing? Or is one's goodness erased by a moral blemish?

Think of some people today, those who genuinely care about goodness. Think of some respected philanthropists, leaders, intellectuals, celebrities, or artists. Some hold opinions we might believe as morally wrong or evil, but we still acknowledge their virtues and goodness. They aren't bad people just because of their single opinion on abortion, politics, or whether they eat meat or not. Yet you can still have a disagreement.

When we look to the past of human civilization, there have been many evils committed. We have a tendency to analyze these evils and ascribe their cause to something that may appear to be evil, but isn't necessarily aimed at evil. Look at authoritarianism. Fascists, Nazis, and Stalinists were authoritarians. But so are those who call for martial law during times of chaos. So are those who drag a person from their home because the laws they've broken warrant prison time. Same with those who oppose me driving my car while under the influence of drugs or alcohol. Authoritarianism is the case in all those who in many situations say, "you are not allowed to freely do something because it does not aim at the good." Although some authoritarians have committed unspeakable atrocities, authoritarianism is not necessarily aiming at what is evil. Nor is the pro-life, conservative, liberal, communist, meat eater, leftist, or anti-vaxxer aimed at what is evil.

If this is true, then in the same manner, the colonialist, racist, homophobe, and sexist, weren't necessarily aimed at evil either. Some of these people made valuable contributions to our conception of goodness, virtue, and the highest ideals a human life should strive for. Although Aristotle seemed to support a type of slavery,[68] he also offered insightful teachings on ethics. Although Martin Luther King Jr. cheated on his wife and had several affairs,[69] he undeniably stood for justice and human dignity. Although Jesus was against divorce and remarrying,[70] he offered great teachings on love. Although Gandhi so admirably opposed colonialism, for at least part of his life he seemed to espouse racism.[71] Although the American founding fathers owned slaves,[72] they made great advances to our understanding of democratic government and human liberty. Although Marx was an antisemite,[73] he furthered our understanding of workers' rights and labour laws.

Just because someone held a different moral view than we do, doesn't mean they weren't trying to aim at the good. Sometimes we lose sight of the good and focus on the shadow it casts instead. Marx, Gandhi, and the founding fathers wouldn't agree on every moral issue, but they are all worthy of respect and admiration because the merits of their virtues demand praise. The good from these figures outweigh the bad.

Perhaps historical figures are the same way. Perhaps *our* historical figures are the same way. Statues of our historical figures were erected to commemorate a higher light that is not always extinguished by their darkness. They should not be torn down because that's not why they were put up.

And even if we shouldn't have statues and we should just tear them all down, then what are we building a monument to in their place? What values are we idolizing? What ideals are we striving towards that we publicly commemorate? Without figures or archetypes to act as an exemplar of virtue, how are we to embody goodness? If we tear down our statues and despise our ancestors, then where are we to know virtue? How are we to know goodness? Are we to extinguish a torch from the past while thinking we are no longer in darkness?

If we are to identify the evils of our past, we must also identify the ideals of our future. From our past, we must take what was good, noble, and right, while discarding what was evil, ruinous, and devastating. To do this, we must extract that which is good if we are to destroy that which is bad.

We must understand that an actor will play both heroes and villains throughout their career. The heroic acts don't make them less of a villain, just as the villainous acts don't make them less of a hero. Often the young revolutionaries fighting for goodness will grow into the corrupt elite whom the future generation will battle against in the name of progress. If we purge the villains from our past, we must first identify what made them heroes.

Destruction in the service of goodness will fail to yield goodness with destruction alone. For Ares cannot create or give life, he can only destroy. We must supplement our forces of destruction with forces of creation. If we are to destroy the statues of our past heroes, then we must erect monuments to the good they were meant to embody. To tear down evil, we must also create goodness. It's time we ask ourselves which values and virtues we want to idolize. Without a light to guide our steps, we walk in darkness.

Do we Deserve Freedom?

Freedom is not the ultimate ideal of humanity. What we should be aiming at is goodness, prosperity, and human flourishing. The opportunity for freedom and liberty can be in service to this aim. The freedom of a people can allow for the human spirit to soar to new heights and create magnificent works of beauty beyond one's imagination. However, without proper guidance, freedom can open the door for the human spirit to create horrors and suffering beyond one's most terrifying nightmares.

Freedom is a double-edged sword that can serve both light and darkness. The blade of liberty must be tempered with wisdom or else the kingdom will come crashing down upon us. When you look around, do you not see the cracks in the foundation? Do you not see the walls beginning to crumble? A culture would be wise to not impale themselves with the blade they wield.

Where are the wise? Where are those who wisely use their freedom? When you look out onto the masses, is it obvious that wisdom and virtue are our guides? Or have we lost our way and become fat, seated upon the prosperity of our ancestors? The day wisdom and virtue fall from the common tongue is the day I tremble at the freedom we hold.

The merits of freedom depends on the moral character of a people. Is our moral character worthy of freedom? Do we deserve freedom? Can we handle it? Like giving a loaded handgun to a child, can we trust ourselves with the freedom we hold so dear? Freedom is a great power, and we've been told that with great power comes great responsibility. Are we responsible enough to be free? Can we trust ourselves to navigate the oceans of liberty toward the destination of paradise? Or will our culture land on pleasure island, and forget the original voyage on which we were sent?

Do we not see the storms approaching if we abandon virtue? Do we not see the need for wisdom when steering our ship? Freedom without wisdom will crash our ship onto the rocks. Freedom without virtue will cause our ship to sink under the weight of our own liberty.

Do not confuse my questioning of freedom for a soft support of authoritarianism. As much as I don't want to be aboard a free ship that crashes onto the rocks, I have no desire to be a galley slave where I'm forced to row to an arbitrary destination under the fear of death. But I may not have much of a choice since the survivors of a shipwreck were often rescued and sold into slavery anyway. Perhaps this will be our fate if we crash upon the rocks.

Feelings of Harm and Empathy

We do not want empathy at the expense of excellence. Excellence requires striving and striving needs actors to struggle against one another. Striving is an upward motion, aiming at the heights of what we can become. Although the goal isn't for actors to be harmed during their striving, striving itself shouldn't be limited to mitigate against accidental harm. The goal of excellence is not to prevent harm, but to foster the strive beyond both pleasure and pain.

Currently, in our culture, the lighthouse which directs our moral consideration is shifting towards empathy as our chief moral good. Stopping all feelings of harm and discomfort have become our culture's ultimate moral aim. Concern for one's fellow person is indeed a virtue, but this empathy should not be at the expense of our striving for truth and excellence. Perhaps we are on the right path, though we may be straying off the narrow bridge of virtue into the depths below. I fear we may only realize our blunder when we have gone too far and have passed the torch to a new generation… a new culture that believes their ultimate moral aim is to reduce the harm experienced by others at the expense of excellence and human flourishing.

Hopefully we do not stagnate and forget that the virtue at which we aim lies beyond simply reducing the experience of pain, but in enhancing the spirit of prosperity. Our best nature is when we aim at the shining light beyond our level of articulation, rather than the shadows cast by the objects of our criticism. It is not simply by tearing down statues that we improve our community, but by building monuments and bridges to the best we have to offer.

The Island and the Flood

There once was an island, alone in the sea.
The people built a wall, as tall as could be.
Although they had issues, the island was free.
With a bit of control, as free as could be.

Except there was a minor problem, a fatal failing,
Constant oppression was always prevailing.

On this island were groups, living together.
Some become friends, others, oppressors.

The people got together to oppose the elite,
Some met victory, others, defeat.

Slowly but surely, social change progressed,
Although they strived, people were still oppressed.

But the oceans were rising as they built their wall.
If their dams collapsed, the city would fall.

The walls were maintained by an exploited group.
They unfairly suffered and were left out of the loop.

They were left out of power and political ruling,
Forced the serve masters while their own lives were grueling.

A flood was coming, and the walls needed support.
Without the will of the people, the Island's days would be short.

A cry went up, "Why should we care?"
"Why should the city survive when *they* won't share?"

They pointed at the elite, upon their throne,
Brutal and selfish, corrupt to the bone.

"Why should one laugh while the other must cry?
If the island is flooded, at least the elite will die."

Some people said, "no" and built up the walls.
"Resent feels good until the city falls."

The people held back the flood and stood against Hell.
Although life was unfair, it was still good as well.

And the people came together, at least as many as were needed.
The Island survived and the flood was impeded.

The people stood together and overcame their strife.
They tried to get along and build the Good Life.

With the shared aim of goodwill and hearts for prosperity and peace,
The people tried to be Good, and slowly, the evil ceased.

They were good to their families and good to their friends,
And good to their enemy while making amends.

They were good to themselves and did what they knew should be done.
Although it was hard, each challenge was won.

Though their names are lost, their values survive,
in ancient wisdom that makes cultures thrive.

There's no higher pursuit than good disposition,
And the responsibility to bring Good out of any condition.

As stories of old were understood,
Extract the gold and make it good.

Are You the Hero or the Victim?

If your life was a story, would you be the hero or the victim?

Life has no shortage of misery, tragedy, and suffering. Both the hero and the victim experience the same suffering and hardships. They're both victimized, but the hero refuses to stay a victim while the victim finds their identity in victimhood and suffering. The hero transcends their suffering and rather than identifying with their victimhood, the hero finds their identity in conquering adversity.

Every victimized person I've met has known incredibly tragic circumstances. They've faced horrible suffering and misfortune that I wouldn't wish on anyone. Interestingly though, the most admirable and heroic people I know have also experienced suffering and tragic circumstances... dare I say even comparable. Both the heroes and victims I've seen in the world have known darkness beyond comprehension. But our response to this darkness is what matters.

The fog of darkness comes for us all. The victim cowers in the shadows while the hero stands and moves forward. The victim defines their life through their misery and misfortune, but the hero strives valiantly upwards and onwards. While the victim curses the darkness, the hero creates a light.

Even in victimhood, we can all be heroic. But some of us chose to cling to our circumstances and cry, "This is me." When faced with the option of transcending our situation and rising above the tragedies of life, we're faced with two possibilities: we can define ourselves in our suffering and remain victims, or we can define ourselves as one who moves forward heroically in spite of our suffering and triumphs over darkness.

How to Build a Dynasty

So, you want to start a dynasty, eh?

Although the days of traditional warlords such as Genghis Khan and Alexander the Great are behind us, you can still build your dynasty according to modern rules. For those of you who aren't familiar with a dynasty, think of it as a powerful club of your friends and family who control society (for the better, of course). Every human civilization saw an elite group of people, dynasties, who possessed a disproportionate level of power and influence. Our society today is no different. Even though social change and progress have occurred throughout history, there have always been elite groups at the top of society throughout these transitions. This guide will equip you with how the create a dynasty that'll be a ruling player in your country and culture for generations to come.

While everyone else is sitting around watching Netflix, you'll have to work hard if you want to create a dynasty. You'll have to be a part of the elite, which means you need to work to earn money. Contrary to popular belief, this is possible. You'll just have to work for it.

The first thing to do with your money is to get into real estate. Acquire land—lots of it. Property is the oldest form of wealth and the foundation for any great dynasty. You'll want to be a landowner rather than someone who just works and rents the land. To build your influence, you need to have property.

The West, generally speaking, protects property rights as the foundation of legal society. Without the state assuring that the property of businesses and individuals is secure, investment into the country would be a risky gamble. The state can't afford to not protect property rights, so get yourself into the protected club. I'd recommend learning the property laws of your country and state to ensure you understand how the system works to best protect your fundamental asset.

Property is power. Not only is your land ownership protected by the state, but you also have a place to live for free once you own the land. Often you'll have to pay property tax, but this fee will be minimal compared to the income you can earn from your property.

Renting your property to others is an effective way to earn cash. If you're looking for other ways to earn money through property, you can also develop the land for agricultural, industrial, or business purposes.

Along with land, you need money to build your dynasty. You can't always rely on your property to generate income, so it's good to diversify into other investments.

You have to remember that money itself is worthless, it's the goods that money can buy that have value. Acquire the things of value rather than hoarding cash. You'll want to avoid having too much money in savings. This isn't helping you make more money, and if anything, you're losing wealth since inflation is eating up the value of your savings.

Other investments you should consider are shares of profitable companies, stocks that pay dividends, mutual funds, precious metals, and cryptocurrencies.

It'll also help if you own a business that generates further income. You'll want to register your business as a corporation as soon as possible. Being a corporation allows you the benefit of being taxed in a lower tax bracket, various loopholes for tax deductibles expenses, and also shields you and your business partners from personal liability since the Western legal system recognizes corporations as distinct legal entities.

Once you've solidified your place as an economic powerhouse, you'll want to enter the political realm. With enough money, you can "influence" politicians and political parties with generous donations to their election campaigns. Funding lobby groups will also be effective in pressuring the government to support your desired policies.

It will also help to become involved with a specific political party. With your accomplishments in business and deep pockets, you'll go a long way in the party. Soon enough you'll be influencing the party platform, policy, and strategy, maybe even taking a leadership position, unless you want to work in the shadows.

While you're involved in politics, it's crucial to pay attention to public education. Who controls the schools controls the next generation. Who controls the next generation controls the future. Using your power and influence, mold the education system according to the values you see fit. Slowly but surely, adjust the curriculum content to further your cultural objectives and work diligently to get the right people in the right administrative positions.

You'll also need to mold the culture outside of the classroom. To enhance your dynasty's influence, the next step should be to acquire a media outlet. "News companies" aren't just news, they're a means of information distribution. In the words of George Orwell, "Knowledge is power."[74] Not only power for you, but power over others. As the owner of a media outlet, you can choose the information you want your audience to see to shape the worldview of the masses. This will further your political objectives and continually grow your influence.

Once the media is under your control, set your sights on The Academy and academic institutions. Make sure the "experts" are singing the tunes of your choice. Fund scientific studies, research organizations, and academic institutions that align with your desired ideology. Using your political influence, gradually insert people into the academic setting who are sympathetic to your goals. Use your media outlets to provide a mouthpiece for whatever topics will solidify the academic consensus you wish to pursue.

At this point, it would be wise to familiarize yourself with the common people. Truthfully, you should always keep the common people on your side. Involve yourself in the community to understand the masses and show yourself as a virtuous benefactor. If you're seen as a generous and charitable figure who prioritizes the community, you will be loved by the people. If you allow yourself to be a part of the community, you will know the common tongue. It is crucial to keep yourself from becoming disconnected and elitist. Not only is it a troubling look, but you separate yourself from the knowledge of your culture. Understanding the people and current trends is important if you want to maintain your influence.

While involving yourself in the community, be mindful of the various religions and spiritual traditions. Insert yourself into religious communities and become a friend of the faith. Learn wisdom from spiritual traditions and adjust your narrative to resonate with particular religions. Human beings are profoundly spiritual, whether religious or not. If your dynasty can strike a spiritual chord in the masses, there will be a divine force behind your support.

Now that you're a major player in the economy, government, education, media, and community, your dynasty has considerable influence. To grow your influence and become an unstoppable force, you should then focus your sights on sports and entertainment. Local sports teams and movies aren't just a fun night out, they're an opportunity for your dynasty to shape the hearts and minds of a culture. Consider buying a sports team to have access to the fans. You keep them distracted with games while selecting the advertisements and subtle political messages they're exposed to. Owning a sports team allows you to take the pulse of a community which can prove immensely valuable.

Also, consider funding the production of movies and influencing which stories are created to control the cultural narrative. People perceive the world through stories. The Greek philosopher, Plato, thought that myths and storytelling should be reserved for the ruling elite due to the power that art and stories have over the minds of a culture.[75] Promote stories that further the philosophical objectives of your dynasty and you will mold the narrative of a population without them realizing it.

Above all, make sure you take care of your people. It's unwise to make enemies when friends are much more fruitful. If those that work for you are well compensated and have no reason for resentment, they will love you and be grateful. In ancient Rome, generals would pay their armies from their personal fortune, this would ensure the loyalty and devotion of their soldiers. When a general would compensate their soldiers well, they would side with their general over their allegiance to Rome.

Speaking of soldiers, a dynasty must have teeth. Since you're now a very important person, it would be wise to hire a private security team. But private security won't be enough to secure your dynasty when the waves get rough. Use your power and influence to make friends with high-ranking generals and chiefs of staff. In the event of social unrest or political instability, you'll want to be on the side of the military rather than looking down the barrel of their weapons. In times of peace, your soldiers will be dollar signs and media headlines. In times of conflict, you'll be glad you have connections with the military apparatus.

And finally, aim your dynasty's ambitions at the common good. Serve peace, prosperity, and human flourishing. Remember, dynasties collapse more often from internal decay than external attack. Revolutions are born out of injustice, extreme inequality, and corrupt governance. If you want to build a successful dynasty, strive valiantly toward the conditions that will discourage a population from rebelling.

The Eternal Elite

Warlords, monarchs, lords and nobles, the rich and powerful—*the elite*. Even in communist and socialist states that have tried to remove the private accumulation of wealth and elitism, there still exists the elite among the ranks of the government and the military. The elite never disappears, the elite only changes form.

There has always been an elite. There have always been people on top, people who have more than others, people who hold more power. Even in egalitarian societies where equality was pursued with respect to wealth and opportunity, there were some people who held a disproportionate amount of influence over their society. Social groups demand hierarchy. This is human nature. This is inevitable.

Across any given domain, people will vary in their ability, and some will rise to the top. With a skill, there will be people who are better or worse at performing this skill. Those who are better at something get compensated more. They become the elite. In the art of money-making and commerce, there are people who are better and worse. The ones who are better earn more money, resources, and influence, becoming the elite. Even in a society without money, there are those who are better connected, more charismatic, or have more resources than others, causing one to have more influence over their society, becoming the elite.

We can never get rid of the elite. The financial elite may disappear, but they'll re-emerge using a different currency. The elite will always be in power. This is an eternal truth. The moment we stop trying to get rid of the elite and start focussing on influencing the elite to be good is the moment we start doing political philosophy.

There has always been an elite, and there always will be an elite. We should not focus on how to get rid of the elite, instead, we should focus on how to join them. If there will always be an elite, then to a certain extent, we have the moral obligation to become the elite. The elite holds a tremendous amount of power over a society. Why not join them? Why not ascend from your position and use your elevated power to bring good into the world?

Anyone Can Become Wealthy

You've heard it said, "The rich get richer, and the poor get poorer." This is not true. In fact, anyone can become rich. Although this is not professional financial advice, it seems that with the proper knowledge and habits, anyone can become wealthy. Unless faced with tragedy or financial disaster, even those earning minimum wage can become wealthy beyond their imagination.

The secret? Compound interest.

...

In ancient China, there lived an arrogant emperor who liked to travel around the country boasting his skills. He would embarrass and humiliate people as he challenged them to various games. No one could refuse. After all, who could deny an emperor? To encourage his competitors, the emperor would promise them any prize they desired. Being a wealthy ruler, he could afford his occasional loss.

While on his travels, the emperor searched a city market for someone to beat in a game. He spotted a lowly merchant and challenged him to a game of chess. Little did the emperor know, this merchant enjoyed chess and was quite good. To the Emperor's surprise, he was defeated by the merchant. Although arrogant, the emperor was a man of his word. As promised, he asked the merchant to name his prize. Being a simple man, the merchant asked the emperor for a payment of rice every day for each square on the chessboard. But the merchant was a clever man. He asked that for each day, the rice payment be doubled, starting with one grain of rice. The emperor looked at the merchant and laughed. "You fool. You could ask me for anything, and you ask for rice? I accept your small request and pity your simple mind."

The next day, the merchant received his payment of one grain of rice. Then two grains, then four, then eight, and so on, doubling each day. The emperor soon learned how fast one grain of rice could double. On the 14th day, the merchant received a payment of 8192 grains of rice. On the 21st day, he received over *one million* grains of rice. After the fortieth day, the merchant was entitled to over a trillion grains of rice. There wasn't enough rice throughout the entire kingdom to pay the merchant and the emperor became known as a fool.

This is the secret of compound interest.

If you invest just 6 dollars a day for 40 years, you'll have over a million dollars. Just 6 dollars a day. If you invest 16 dollars a day for the same period of time, you'll have nearly 3 million dollars to your name.[76]

How does this work?

Investments. Investments grow wealth. From the smallest seed, investments can grow into the largest tree. And these trees come in different forms. Bonds, stocks, and mutual funds are the most common types of investments and are sufficient to make anyone wealthy over time.

Bonds are essentially a way of loaning money to the government. Just as people borrow money through a bank or credit card, governments borrow money from investors with an agreement to pay the money back with interest. Bonds are considered extremely safe since the government promises they will be paid back. The only way a bond would not be paid back is if the government collapsed, which is highly unlikely. Due to the high safety of this investment type, the interest earned from bond payments are fairly low, with an annual return ranging on average from 1% to 5%.

Stocks, on the other hand, are riskier than bonds while offering a higher average annual return of over 10%. Owning stock is to directly own a piece of a company. This is why stocks are also referred to as "shares" because to own them is to own a share of a company. When a company wants to raise money, they can calculate what their business is worth and sell ownership of their company to the public. This is when a company is considered a "public company" or "publicly traded company" because anyone in the public can own a piece of that company. The price of a company's stock then changes depending on the value of the company in the eyes of investors. If people like a company and think it is a well-performing business, the share price usually goes up. If a company isn't doing well and looks to be going downhill, then the share price usually declines. This is because people buy or sell shares depending on if they want to own that company. Although stocks can increase and decrease in price, you only get paid for the stock once you chose to sell.

Stocks don't have any value in themselves. At the end of the day, they are just a piece of a company. If that company becomes worthless and claims bankruptcy, then a piece of that company is also worthless. But when a company is doing well, its stock price is worth money. In some cases, lots of money. A stock is worth money because people want to own it. The better the company, the more people will pay for the stock. So long as a company is doing well, people will want to own a part of that company as a means of storing value. That's why it's important to do research on a company before investing.

Mutual funds are a great way to combine the safety of bonds with the high profits of stocks. A mutual fund is a collection of stocks. When you buy shares of a mutual fund, what you're really buying is pieces of multiple companies. In some cases, hundreds of companies. The people who operate mutual funds invest in many different companies and put all these shares into a collection. When you invest in mutual funds, you invest in the whole collection of businesses rather than individual companies. This way, your investments are diversified; so, if one company in the fund goes bankrupt, then you don't lose all of your money. They're called "mutual funds" because they're a mutual benefit to you and the investment organization. When the stocks in the fund increase in value, both you and the financial organization benefit. The organization that manages the fund usually takes between 1-3% of your profits as a management fee to pay their employees and keep the lights on. This way, the organization selling the mutual funds has the incentive to earn you money.

When you make money, so do they. The more money their investments earn you, the more money they keep.

To highlight the safety and profitability of mutual funds, consider the S&P 500. The S& 500 is a list of the top 500 largest companies in the American economy and this list is constantly being updated. Since the American economy is the largest economy in the world, businesses in the S&P 500 are often international companies. Investing in the S&P 500, which is to invest in the top 500 companies in the American economy, is a great way to diversify your investments across top-performing businesses. While it's true that in times of economic downturns, like recessions and depressions, the stock price of even the best companies will decrease. But overall, there are more good years than bad years, and downturns are always met with increases. After factoring in periods of recessions and depressions for the past 100 years, the S&P 500 has increased an average of 10.5% per year.

Figure 5: S&P 500 Index – 90-Year Historical Chart of the S&P 500 stock market index since 1927. Historical data is inflation-adjusted using the headline CPI and each data point represents the month-end closing value. From, https://www.macrotrends.net/2324/sp-500-historical-chart-data

Whether you invest in bonds, stocks, or mutual funds, the goal is to put your money into assets that increase in value. Then if you can manage it, reduce your expenses, increase your income, and invest more money into assets that will earn you more money. Additionally, rental properties, businesses, and dividends are other ways to generate more income/cash flow.

Rental properties are buildings you own but rent out to tenants. Being a landlord can be profitable, although it will cost money to repair and maintain the properties. Investing in start-ups or private businesses can be profitable when the business succeeds. Lastly, dividends are payments that companies give shareholders on a monthly, quarterly, or annual basis as payment for owning a piece of that company. Since shareholders own pieces of a company, they often have some say in how the company operates through voting rights. Oftentimes shareholders will pay themselves a portion of the company's revenue in the form of a dividend. This can be a great way to earn money from stocks without having to sell.

Money-making has been an art since the dawn of trade and commerce. There are plenty of ways to earn money beyond just your paycheck. While the poor squander their money on things that lose their value over time, the rich invest their money into assets that increase in value over time. Investing your paycheck into investments can increase your income and overall wealth, taking you from surviving to thriving and joining the ranks of the elite.

...

Although it should be noted, true wealth is found in the heart, not in the bank account. One can have all the money in the world and still be miserable. Wealth should not be put on a pedestal and regarded as the meaning of one's life. Wealth can serve as a tool to take care of one's necessities, such as shelter, food, and clothing, and provide us with luxuries and vacations. But wealth cannot buy one meaning and long-term fulfillment. The initial joy of a new purchase wears off, leaving one feeling empty and dissatisfied. Wealth cannot buy genuine friendships. Wealth cannot replace the warmth of human relationships. Wealth cannot bring our loved ones back to life. Cherish the important things in life because they cannot be bought with money.

Wealth should be used as a tool to enhance the life of one's family, friends, and community. Wealth should be used as a tool to create good things in this world and to support those who have less.

Excellence Over Equality

Making things equal does not make things better. Equality is a horizontal consideration while excellence is an upward striving. We should individually focus on the pursuit of excellence over concerns of equality. Equality itself does not create the good things of life, it just spreads them out. Equality, while in some cases being a praiseworthy virtue, is anti-creative. It does not create, it just redistributes what has already been created.

We shouldn't want everyone to be equal, we should want everyone to be better off than they were before. We should want to raise everyone up rather than levelling everyone out. In theory, equality can go either up or down. Those with more can become less, or those with less can become more. When the height of pillars are unequal, either the shorter heights can be made higher or the higher heights can be made shorter. If our goal is equality, then the direction of our equality doesn't matter. So long as the height of the pillars are equal, it doesn't matter if the pillars are small or large.

But this is wrong. I say that we should want higher pillars over lower ones. We should want people raised up rather than brought down. We should want greatness, prosperity, and excellence over the lesser qualities of life, even if these lesser qualities are spread equally.

The radical striving for equality often ignores the force that drives conditions upwards. If equality is to be a virtue, then it must be an equality of an upward trajectory. It must be a type of equality that lifts people up to new heights rather than toppling that which is above.

The issue is insufficiency, not disparity. Equality wouldn't matter if everyone had *enough*. If everyone had enough money, resources, and opportunities, then it shouldn't matter if one person has more than another. Unless you're angry that someone has more than you. In this case, the will for equality is resentment and jealousy. Rather than being resentful of someone for having more than you do, be discontent with yourself for having less and use this passion as an incentive to rise above where you are now.

Strangely, some people want equality as if it were their birthright. They think their existence entitles them to an equal share of the good things of this world without having to put in the work.

Equality originated as a political right: equality under the law, equal rights to vote, equal rights to freedom and opportunity, and equal access to earning wealth and acquiring property. In a world where some people are barred from these fundamental rights, equality is a virtue we should strive for.

But full equality? Equality of resources and happiness? This is worse than a fantasy. It is an impossibility that makes things worse when strived for.

History has shown that when equality becomes an economic goal, poverty, suffering, social and collapse is the only result. Look at Russia, Cuba, Venezuela, China, North Korea, and other countries who've been possessed by the desire to punish the wealthy and bring full equality to their people. Turns out, when a culture becomes focussed on redistributing the gains of those better-off, incentive is lost, the upward momentum is shattered, and society collapses only to set the conditions for a brutal authoritarian regime to take power. Even when these regimes continue with the goal of equality, it's an equality of poverty and misery shared by the masses.

Equality itself does not contain the seeds for flourishing. Equality does not grow, it just trims the trees that grow too high. Equality does not shine, it just dims the light of those more luminous. Equality does not build, it just tears down that which is higher than the rest. The worst kind of equality is the political will of the bitter and resentful. They care more about tearing down those who have more rather than lifting up those who have less.

I offer you a new kind of equality. An equality not obsessed with outcome, but with opportunity. An equality that recognizes in everyone the capacity to ascend to new heights no matter their starting point. An equality that doesn't care where you start, but encourages the actions and attitudes that lead to a better place.

The focus on 'leveling the playing field' detracts from the upward momentum of prosperity. People should strive for the best. They should strive for virtue, prosperity, and excellence of character. But when people strive, some will do better than others. And some will stumble along the path. Over time, distance will emerge between the climbers closer to excellence and those farther away. The important thing is to keep our sights on the shining heights of the mountain that we strive towards rather than creating a valley of equality. Ascension is the aim, not equality. Growth is the goal, not equality. Excellence is the pursuit of the thriving person, not the jealous and resentful cry for equality.

The Sickness of Safety

And these searchers of safety...

They find things outside of their control, and they try to control them. They try to protect us from the things that cause us harm. They want to help.

But sometimes they go too far.

Life is good. Life could be better, but it could be a hell of a lot worse too. Generally speaking, we live in an age of peace and plenty. We have no Great War. No Great Depression. Life is pretty good. But therein lies the problem. We have no rallying point. No common cause. No opposition to struggle against. With whom do we wage war when we have no enemy? What happens when we have no harm to contend against?

When we have no pressing harm, we set our sights on harm itself. When we have no immediate threat, we become obsessed with eliminating threats wherever they are. When we are living in times of safety, we wage war against injury and personal harm.

For some folks, they become obsessed with safety. Safety becomes paramount, occupying their top priority. Their life is a crusade against the possibility of harm. They suffer from a constant disease of fear and worry about all things rather than facing life with a courageous and heroic stance.

We are a sick culture—a people who long for safety and security above all else. We have a pathological need for some structure and authority to tell us what we can and can't do lest we hurt others or even ourselves. We would cut off our hands so they're safe from slivers and paper cuts.

In addition to the modern world's need for safety, there's a need for the *performance* of safety. It often doesn't matter if something is actually safe, so long as it appears safe and soothes the afflicted. When those suffering from the sickness of safety are shown the uselessness of the antidotes they cling to, they will deny it, collapsing into themselves and retreating further into their fear.

They do not want their delusions destroyed. They would rather build a wall against fear than face it with courage. For courage is not the absence of fear, but acting in spite of fear. Courage is not just a virtue, but is the root of heroism and the fulfillment of humanity's ancient myth. Through fear, is fulfillment. Through danger, is achievement. Through courage, is the life-giving spirit that builds human civilization.

But those plagued with the obsession for safety know nothing of courage. They are scared and try to build themselves a monument to their fear. They cover themselves in cushions and bubble wrap so the world won't hurt them as they decay into their comfort and safety. To live in a hamster ball would be ideal for these people, preferring to be padded and protected from the outside world. Only this wouldn't satisfy their need for safety. Their sickness would remain incurred. For even in a ball, the dis-eased could still find harm with the outside world.

While physically protected from the harm of the world, the dis-eased will find fault with how the world makes them feel. They will begin their crusade to create a world that makes them feel safe, rather than becoming the kind of people who can face a dangerous world and triumph over it. When they can't bubble-wrap themselves from harm, they begin to bubble-wrap the world. They make it their mission to remove all the sharp edges and threats of life so their safety can be undisturbed.

The world is dangerous. Life is inherently threatening. The desire to bubble wrap the world and make life harm-free is an impossible ambition. And if it were possible, if the possibility of harm was permanently eliminated and life itself became totally safe, we would inflict harm on ourselves just to give us something to contend against.

The human being needs harm. The human spirit needs threats and dangers to encounter. Without danger, we become weak and wither away. The fulfilled person strives against these harms. Like a sword, we must be forged through fire. Like a diamond, becoming our ideal is formed through heat and pressure.

The Athenians of ancient Greece, a prosperous people, were renowned for their rejection of safety and comfort. Athens was a major force throughout the Mediterranean, boasting a massive fleet, robust trade networks, and an influential culture that spread across the known world.[77] What accounts for their success? It wasn't their obsession with safety, that's for sure. The Greek politician Pericles famously said, "Our daring has forced a path to every land and sea, erecting timeless memorials to itself everywhere for good and ill."[78] Like every great civilization, the Athenian appetite for danger was the seeds to their prosperity. The Athenians knew the sentiment of John A. Shedd, "A ship in harbour is safe, but that is not what ships are built for."[79] Although people are safest in the security of their beds, that's not what human beings were built for. We are a species of pioneers and explorers, a species of warriors and survivors. We are a species who evolved by facing our fears, standing courageously against a harmful world, and finding prosperity in the dangerous darkness beyond the horizon.

There's irony in the harm that comes from facing too little harm. When life is too safe, everything becomes a threat. This is not the life of a courageous human being, but of a scared rabbit who can never escape its predator. This is the life of someone who can never go anywhere without worry, or without obsession over the safety of their body, mind, and soul. This desperate clinging to life sucks the vitality from our veins. Life then withers and dries up, becoming a hollow shell of what it once was, all to protect oneself against harm and death. All to shelter ourselves from danger of all kinds. We get so scared of danger that we forget how to live. This life we create out of fear is a shadow of what life could be.

Sometimes the sharp edges and bumps of the word will cause death. This is unfortunate but still remains the fate of us all. And what is death anyway if we don't allow ourselves to fully live? In the words of Adlai Stevenson, "It is not how many years are in your life, but the life in your years that count."[80] It doesn't matter how long we live, what matters is what we do with our time while alive. To quote the Roman philosopher Seneca, "There is no reason for you to think that any man has lived long because he has grey hairs or wrinkles; he has not lived long—he has existed long."[81]

What I want for humanity is not to just exist, but to live. I want us to feel the wind on our face and hear the thunder of this world. To live fully, we must risk harm. The life of a scared rabbit is no life for a human being. Death in the face of danger is preferable to a slow and sickly decay.

I suspect that this sickness of safety stems from our fear of death. Many of us are terrified of our own mortality and cling to life, even if they deprive life of everything that makes it worth living. The irony of clinging to a safe life is that you often lose what makes you feel alive. A life solely obsessed with safety is a dull life of the walking dead.

We must make peace with death. We must accept it. We must recognize how death could linger beyond every corner and will eventually greet us all in due time. To borrow another idea from Seneca, "No [one] can have a peaceful life who thinks too much about lengthening it."[82] Once we no longer fear death, we will no longer fear life.

Until then, this fear of death does what fear does best. Fear corrupts and distorts our way of life. Fear makes the world ugly and unbearable. Fear sickens the mind. Fear robs the present of beauty and bliss. Fear is the only feeling that can survive in a mind consumed by the obsession with safety. Fear feeds into the need for control. Fear hangs over one's head like the shadow of death and whispers in our ears the encouragement of our worst impulses. Fear makes the heart cold. Fear warps the soul. And in the words of Franklin D. Roosevelt, "The only thing we have to fear is fear itself."[83]

Those suffering from the sickness of safety work so hard searching for the darkness that sometimes they get scared of their own shadow. Our shadow will always be with us. Wherever we go, there will always be the possibility of danger. There will always be darkness in the light. There will always be harm in the harmony. The goal isn't to eliminate all harm, but to become the kind of person who can withstand the harm of this world and triumph.

Our Species' Top Priority

The Health of The Environment & The Health of Those in Their Environment
What's more important: the environment's wellbeing or the prosperity of humanity?

We live on a planet containing life and vibrant ecosystems. It is a primary ethical priority to strive for the thriving of life. However, it seems that too much concern for the wellbeing of our planet can be harmful to human life.

Before we begin, we should rip off the Band-Aid of climate alarmism. Things are going to be okay. It's not the end of the world. Even in the most severe predictions, humanity will survive. As the Earth warms, areas that become too hot are balanced by new areas that are melting and becoming habitable. Humans have migrated for the entirety of our history, and we will adapt to future migration. We will rise to the occasion of whatever threatens our civilization. Our technology to produce food has increased exponentially which will supplement food sources that could be potentially affected by climate change.[84] There are more trees on Earth today than there were 100 years ago,[85] and the earth is greener today than it was 30 years ago.[86] Since the year 2000, developed countries have been consistently reducing their carbon emissions.[87] Engines and carbon emissions are continuing to be made more efficient as we improve our technology.[88] Since 1975, the CO_2 emissions of the average vehicle have been cut in half due to innovation and development in the industry.[89] Increasing efforts have been made to clean up the garbage from our oceans, with astonishing success.[90] International consensus is being reached to stop overfishing our oceans.[91] Breakthrough technologies are continually being developed to benefit our environment, such as an enzyme created by scientists in 2020 that breaks down plastic in just a few hours.[92] And not to mention the development of nuclear fusion technology that will provide humanity with unlimited clean energy, effectively phasing out fossil fuels.[93]

We're going to be okay. But this hasn't stopped the dark side of environmentalism that displaces human wellbeing as the most important ethical objective. Climate change is happening and human beings have an influence on the wellbeing of our planet, but it's crucial we remain grounded in facts and cautious optimism rather than diving into the destruction of doomsday thinking. Again, we're going to be okay. We always have been. Humanity will find a way as we always have.

The reason why we're distressed by climate change is because we view it as a threat to us human beings. We are the reason why we care about climate change. The environment should not be our top priority. Human wellbeing and the prosperity of human communities should be our top priority.

Oftentimes human flourishing includes a harmonious and sustainable relationship with our environment. However, this environmentalism is not for the sake of our environment alone, but for the sake of human beings as well. It is important to clarify this distinction between priorities. Some environmentalists view environmental concerns as necessary for human survival. While another school of thought believes the environment is important for its own sake. The former places human wellbeing as the top priority, while the latter places human wellbeing beneath the wellbeing of the environment. If we consider the environment as our top priority, then human wellbeing becomes a secondary value. When discussing ethics and the best path forward, the wellbeing of humans and the striving for prosperity is the chief priority. To do otherwise is to consider the concerns of people as beneath an objective independent of human wellbeing.

An argument can be made that harmony with our environment is the best course of action for the sustainability of human civilization. The key to this environmentalism is that it places human wellbeing at the center of our ethical concerns. This is not to deny the importance of environmental concerns. The environment is important. And the environment is only important because it is necessary for prosperity and human wellbeing.

The past several decades have seen the rapid growth of Western environmentalism. Although cultures and philosophies that give ethical consideration to their environment are common throughout history, we're witnessing the birth of a uniquely Western environmental movement—with religious intensity. Originating in North America and Europe at the same time religious affiliation is on the decline, environmentalism provides a worldview and a value structure to fill the cultural void in the absence of religion. The fundamental priority of human wellbeing seems forgotten in some Western environmental circles. Particularly in the more radical kind.

Whereas some cultures in the past have viewed their environment as an ethical concern, modern environmentalists seem to consider care for the environment as *the* ethical concern. These advocates seem to hold the environment's health as their fundamental ethical objective. While there's nothing wrong with caring about the health of our environment and local ecosystems, placing environmental values above the concerns for human wellbeing is counterproductive to the goals of a just and prosperous society.

Yes, the environment should be an ethical concern. But it's not *the* ethical concern. The environment is not the most important thing. Human beings and the wellbeing of our communities are the most important thing. When the environment is considered as the most important ethical objective, the needs and concerns of humans take a backseat to an ideology devoted to the health of our planet above the health of human beings.

Of course, the health of our environment impacts the wellbeing of humans. Famines are not good for our community. Let's prevent those. Smog and toxic air quality that leads to adverse health effects should be avoided. Overfishing our oceans to the point of extinction of our species' most widely consumed food source also seems like a bad long-term solution for human wellbeing. These environmental concerns place human needs at the heart of the discussion, as they should be. The advancement of wellbeing, prosperity, and human flourishing are the focal points of ethical consideration, not the health of our environment. Let's not forget this.

When it comes down to it, the needs of human beings are more important for our ethical deliberation. Unnecessary suffering of non-human life should be avoided. But when it comes down to the needs of human communities versus the needs of plants, animals, and the climate, human needs seem to be more important. This is not to say we should abuse our pets and clear-cut forests willy-nilly. But if a situation comes down to "saving the turtles" or saving the 3.2 million people who die annually from inhaling smoke from wood-burning stoves that could be avoided by adopting fossil fuels such as oil or gas,[94] then the turtles can respectfully wait their turn. And if there are no turtles left, then they will join the ranks of 99.9% of all species that ever existed on Earth that no longer exist.[95]

On the topic of implementing fossil fuel production, it isn't always more negative for the environment. In the case above of wood-burning stoves, it should also be remembered that burning wood also releases carbon into the atmosphere while requiring tremendous deforestation and destruction to local ecosystems to maintain the demand of people who burn wood for heating and cooking. Switching wood-burning stoves to fossil fuel energy sources can have benefits for the environment. While natural gas is harmful to the environment, burning natural gas is less harmful to the environment than burning coal or oil, and is currently more feasible than renewable resources.[96] In fact, the United States has decreased their carbon emissions output by replacing coal and oil with natural gas.[97] However, since natural gas is harmful to the environment and does not fit with the tenants of radical Western environmentalism, environmental advocates refuse to acknowledge the nuance of environmental considerations through their opposition to natural gas initiatives and paint all fossil fuels with the same broad brushstroke. This is evident by the environmentalists' opposition to implementing hydraulic fracking technologies[98] (a cleaner method of extracting natural gas), which has been shown to decrease carbon emissions when replacing coal and oil.[99]

It's also interesting to note the difference in scope between the modern Western environmental movement and the environmentally conscious cultures of the past. For example, environmentalists often cite the relationship between Indigenous peoples and their environment as an ideal the Industrial West should aspire towards. Indigenous peoples held great respect for their environment and regarded themselves as its stewards. They would thank the spirit of the wildlife they killed for food, used the entirety of the animal to avoid wasting their sacrifice, and tried to live in harmony with their resources rather than dominating nature.[100] This Indigenous environmentalism is radically different from modern Western environmental movements. Whereas Indigenous environmentalism cared about their environment as a priority, Western environmentalists care about *the* environment as *the* priority. Harmony is the goal, not radicalism. Environmental goals have transcended local considerations for ecosystems, air quality, and wildlife, to focus on the health of the Earth as a whole. Environmental considerations are no longer one ethical goal among many. Rather, environmentalists consider most environmental concerns to be the most important value, above concerns for human wellbeing.

The more radical environmentalists advocate for banning non-electric cars, planes, cattle farming, single-use plastic and non-recyclable materials, fossil fuel usage, and even fireworks.[101] It doesn't matter the good that comes from these technologies—if something harms the environment, it should be banned, in the view of modern environmentalists. If something's not recyclable, it should not be produced, regardless of the good it can provide our species, say the radical environmentalists. However, I suppose that when our quality of life inevitably erodes due to the restriction of the needs and luxuries we enjoy, at least we can take solace in our commitment to the environment. The environmental gods will smile on our sacrifice.

The Western environmentalist movement also seems to disdain the advancements of industrial society. The creation of automobiles, air conditioning, pharmaceutical medications, and industrial farming, to name a few technologies, have contributed to the most peaceful and prosperous period in human history.[102] And not just for people living in North America and Europe. Millions of people are being lifted out of poverty around the globe every year thanks to our technological advancements. In fact, according to the World Bank as of 2022, each day for the past twenty-five years, over one hundred thousand people have risen out of poverty thanks to the progress of humanity.[103] This is unprecedented in human history and is a cause for celebration. Western environmental movements seek to undermine this improvement in human life. They seem to believe that the health of our environment is *more* important than the goodness and prosperity of human life. Let environmental initiatives come, but not at the expense of human flourishing.

Of course, it's easy for Western environmentalists to see the big picture from the mountain on which we view the world. Only this mountain isn't natural. This mountain is forged from iron and steel. Industry and production have forged this mountain with blood and sweat bathing the foundations. Fossil fuel combustion and electricity production have propelled our rise to the top, and now Western environmentalists dare to look down to the valley below and discourage the use of the technologies that have made us prosper.

This sentiment is best expressed by India's Environment Minister, Bhupender Yadav, at the 2021 United Nations climate change conference.

"How can anyone expect that developing countries make promises about phasing out coal and fossil fuel subsidies? Developing countries still have to deal with their poverty reduction agenda."[104]

Environmentalists want to make the costs of owning a gasoline car unaffordable, while electric options are out of reach for most people. We want to restrict fossil fuel production in our countries, only to import fuel from less environmentally conscious facilities in foreign countries. We want to increase the cost of living for the poorest among us so that the planet can be saved. We want to reduce our carbon emissions and see an unwavering commitment from our allies to the health of our planet at the expense of human flourishing. Our planet's climate and environment are important, insofar as human prosperity is our ultimate ethical aim.

Of course, if humanity destroys its environment, humanity will die. It seems like a harmonious and sustainable relationship with the environment is an important priority, but it is not *the most* important priority. Care for environmental wellbeing is rooted in the more fundamental priority—care for human flourishing and prosperity.

Why Did Jesus Encourage His Followers to Own Swords?

Regardless of what you specifically think of Jesus, he's stirred up quite the conversation over the past 2000 years.

It's curious why someone who preached about peace, tolerance, and justice, also commanded his followers to own weapons of war. In the gospel of Luke, Jesus says to his disciples during their last meal together:

> *"But now if you have a purse, take it, and also a bag; and if you don't have a sword, sell your cloak and buy one."*
>
> *- Luke 22:38 NIV*

Why would a preacher of peace encourage his followers to own weapons of war? This seems like a contradiction.

To understand this idea, we need to consider history. It seems that the underlying threat of force is forever upon us. There have always been those who hold power. And there have always been those who use power for the wrong reasons. But people always hesitate about oppressing and persecuting those with swords. Perhaps Jesus was suggesting that people of peace should be capable of protecting themselves and generating wealth.

At this part of history, Jesus probably knew the local Jewish authorities were coming after him and that he would likely die. His followers would be demonized, arrested, and most likely killed as well. Whether Jesus knew it or not, his followers would set out to preach a new religion that would dominate the coming two thousand years of human history.

Jesus wouldn't have wanted his friends and followers oppressed. He wanted them to live lives of peace and prosperity, and inherit "the kingdom of God," in his words. Perhaps the best way to find peace at this time was to own swords and weapons to protect oneself. After all, as the saying goes, "Walls weren't built because of our friends"—and this seems true for swords as well.

This is not to encourage violence or harm. Violence should be avoided when possible and should always be a last resort for solving any problem. It also should be noted that peaceful solutions are often more effective than violence. In the words of the prophet Muhammad, "The ink of a scholar is worth more than the blood of a martyr."[105] There are far more valuable avenues of empowerment than violent force. Having said this, it's important we also recognize our responsibility to the wellbeing of our community even in extreme circumstances.

If someone always holds the underlying threat of physical force, what is the best thing to do as a person who wants to live in peace? It seems like the best thing to do is to keep in check the power of tyranny. Good people who yearn for peace and justice should be able to stand against those who seek to cause harm.

There are a lot of bad people in the world—more good people than bad people, but there are always a couple of characters who want to cause harm. They're usually pretty scarce, but history shows that they come out of the shadows from time to time.

In a matter of months, your country could be invaded, or maybe your government could fall. The people who once kept you safe might no longer be watching your back when you sleep. Alternatively, your whole financial system could collapse, or a national emergency could be declared, and you'd see the government turn into a police state virtually overnight. This is when a country and its people are put to the test. It's in these moments where the underlying threat of force shows itself to the people. And it's in these moments when we hope that those with force use their power for good rather than harm.

Religious minorities and other oppressed groups certainly know the horrible power a corrupt, tyrannical, and oppressive government can have over their people.

It's in these times of chaos that swords and coin purses are beneficial to one's community. Rather than literally having swords and coin purses, they might be symbols of virtues one should strive for. It seems that swords might be a metaphor for one's capacity for conflict and defense. When one is "armed," metaphorically speaking, they have integrated their aggression for the right reasons and are capable of defending themselves and their community. In keeping with the metaphor, a coin purse represents the mentality and way of life conducive to wealth generation and prosperity.

Perhaps this is what Jesus meant when he encouraged his followers to have a coin purse and obtain a sword. Those with wealth, property, and the ability for defense are more likely to find peace and prosperity than those who hold no wealth, have nothing of their own, and put their swords in the hands of others.

The Real Hero of Batman: Shutting the Door on Tyranny When the Opportunity Comes Knocking

People often regard Batman as the hero of *The Dark Knight*,[106] although there's another hero who's often overlooked. This hero is arguably more heroic than Batman himself.

Although Batman fights for the good and works tirelessly to protect the streets of Gotham, he does so as a vigilante. Batman is a masked figure, operating outside of the law with experimental weapons that would make even law enforcement cringe. With great power comes great responsibility, as they say, and thankfully Batman is guided by a moral compass.

But try as he may, Batman spawns the Joker. In his own words, "You complete me," says the Joker in a conversation with Batman. The Joker is chaos, while Batman is order. Batman strives to put chaos at bay, only to have chaos pushback against his efforts. In a way, Batman is fighting an absurd battle. He and the Joker are locked in the eternal struggle of chaos vs order—anarchy vs structure.

In his confrontation with Joker, Batman (Bruce Wayne) has the resources of wealth and power at his disposal through the technologies of Wayne Enterprises. In *The Dark Knight*, Bruce Wayne unveils a device to hack cellular frequencies and listen to every conversation happening in Gotham City. Spyware so powerful that even the NSA would be impressed. No privacy, no secrets, and all the knowledge of the city at one's fingertips. Knowledge is power, and this machine of absolute knowledge is absolute power.

Bruce Wayne trusts this device with his friend and business colleague, Lucious Fox, to locate the Joker and inform Batman of his whereabouts. In a feat of integrity, Lucious initially turns down the opportunity to use such a powerful machine, believing that too much power in the hands of one person would be devastating. Realizing he has no other choice if they want to locate the Joker and stop his plans to bring death and destruction, Lucious agrees to help, but resigns from Wayne Enterprises so long as this technology exists.

In a more extraordinary testament to virtue and moral courage, Lucious uses the absolute power of the machine, then turns his back on these capabilities. In the most triumphant feat of heroism, Lucious rejects the prospect of absolute power and destroys the machine after Joker has been located.

This wouldn't be the first time in history one person has rejected absolute power. The first President of the United States, George Washington, voluntarily gave up his power after two terms in office, setting the precedent for modern democratic leaders to voluntarily give up power in a peaceful transition of leadership. While we take this act for granted today as it is normal practice in most developed countries, it was far from typical in its historical context. Washington led the Americans in their revolution against the British Empire and has been the only American leader to be elected with unanimous support. There were many people who would have supported Washington as king if he chose that path. Instead, Washington voluntarily rejected the option of absolute power, recognizing the tyranny it creates.[107]

Another historical figure who demonstrated heroic virtue in resisting absolute power was the first Roman dictator, Lucius Quinctius Cincinnatus. In the early days of the Roman Republic, there was no absolute leader. However, in times of extreme emergency, the Romans would elect one man as a dictator, bestowing upon him ultimate power. When an invasion arrived on the doorsteps of Rome, his fellow citizens pleaded Cincinnatus to take the reigns of dictator to defend his country against the invaders. He reluctantly accepted. After the enemy was defeated, Cincinnatus gave up his absolute power and returned to his farm. Cincinnatus is still celebrated today as a beacon of leadership, heroism, and civic virtue.[108]

In the words of Robert G. Ingersoll, "Nearly all men can stand adversity, but if you want to test a man's character, give him power."[109] Power can seduce. Power can corrupt. Power can harden one's heart and possess the mind of the once-righteous. In our quest to vanquish our enemies, it is wise to resist the seductive urge for greater power. When the lust for power awakens in one's soul, a tyrant is born.

It seems that true heroism is stepping back from excessive power rather than embracing it, even if one believes they will use power for the right reasons. It is said, "The path to Hell is paved with good intentions."[110] To recognize in oneself the capacity for corruption is the beginning of leadership.

Blue Zones

There are some places on Earth that are different. Some people might say these places are an exception to the rules, while others might say they are how things should be. What do some communities in Japan, Costa Rica, Greece, and Italy all have in common? These places are known for their populations being happier, healthier, and living much longer than the average human life expectancy. In fact, they have more centurions (people over 100 years old) than anywhere in the world. These areas are called *Blue Zones* and they've been a fascination to scientists and philosophers alike.[111]

What's their secret?

A combination of factors contributes to the success of Blue Zones, according to researchers. It seems that a healthy lifestyle combined with strong relationships are distinct similarities among Blue Zones. People in Blue Zones do the common things expected of a healthy person. They live an active lifestyle, exercise, and eat right. But it's not just lifestyle that causes people to live long and healthy lives.[112]

What is unique about Blue Zones is the people's sense of purpose and their relationships with others. The people who live the healthiest and most fulfilling lives have strong relationships with others, often relationships going back decades. These people also exist in strong communities; they have a purpose they are a part of. Whether it be a career, profession, community group, or shared activity, people with long and fulfilling lives are part of something larger than themselves. It is this sense of purpose that allows one to continue living, especially when our body becomes frail, or when life becomes difficult.

The Okinawans in Japan have a term for this idea, "ikigai", which means, "your purpose for being."[113] If you ask people in Blue Zones why they get up each morning, they often have a deep understanding of their purpose and what they live for. This can be as simple as a grandma living to spend time with her young grandchild, a farmer waking up each morning to provide food for their community, or a fisherman who lives to feed his family.

A strong sense of purpose and community affiliation is contrasted against most modern Western people, who have seen an increase in feelings of loneliness, depression, and nihilism throughout recent decades. According to a Gallup poll, religious affiliation has declined in the West, from 70% of people attending church from 1937 to 2000, to 47% in 2020.[114] Perhaps this accounts for why a poll in 2019 found that 90% of young people in Britain reported feeling that their life lacks meaning.[115] More concerningly, half of American adults report feeling lonely and lacking meaningful relationships.[116]

What could account for this trend of misery and despair? Sociologist Robert Putnam suggests that the decline of community associations are to blame. In his book published in 2000, *Bowling Alone*, Putnam argues that the increase in loneliness, anxiety, and depression among Western countries is correlated with a decline in voluntary community associations.[117] For the past hundred years, popular ways individuals would be involved with a community were through a church, sporting leagues such as baseball or bowling, or even knitting clubs. However, with the spread of television, our community associations declined, leading to an epidemic of loneliness, depression, and misery, further reinforced by the advent of the internet and social media.

Blue Zones seem to suggest that essential to a healthy and fulfilling life is our relationship with others and with our greater community. Prosperity is not known in isolation. If we are to thrive and prosper, we must put ourselves in a community with strong relationships. It is through solitude that we may find our peace, but it is through others that we find our meaning. What good are the joys of life if they cannot be shared with the ones we love?

A Tribute to Love

It might seem sappy to discuss love, that fundamental emotion we compartmentalize in our lives. When we think of human civilization and the force that brings about prosperity, love might not be the first thing that comes to our minds. But we should take a moment and consider love as the cornerstone of the human experience. Where would we be without love? Where would the human species be without the smile from a friend, the embrace of our family, and the warmth from a heart radiating love?

Prosperity, success, human flourishing, and striving towards the kingdom of God are all in vain if the end result is void of love. Love is why we do what we do. Love is why we thrive. Love is what our efforts are all for.

Without love, the world is cold and empty. Without love, no fire burns to keep us warm. The ideal life we want to create for ourselves and for the world is one of love. What good are the fruits of our labour if we can't also enjoy the fruits of our love? Once we arrive at the point where our hard work has paid off and we can enjoy the people and things we love, we realize that love is what keeps us going along the way.

Love, peace, and beauty are goods that justify themselves. They are things we pursue for no other purpose than the experience themselves. Both for our experience and for the experience of others. Love is important and must be one's anchor during the storms of this world. And once the storm clears, our skies are made brighter by the light of love.

But there are those in the world whom the light of love has not illuminated. The warmth of love has not melted the ice in their hearts. It has been said that those who are the hardest to love are those who need it the most. Love is free to give and can uplift those who receive its warmth. Never believe that someone is undeserving of love. A person with enough love in their life is not a person who is coarse and cruel. For whatever they did to not deserve love was done out of coldness and the absence of love's warmth. The solution to an absence of love is not a further lack of love.

There is no greater privilege than to love and be loved. There is no greater obligation than to radiate love wherever we go. Our love for families, friends, romantic partners, and communities are the ties that bind this world. Love is the fire that warms the winters of the world. Love mends and love heals. Love inspires and love motivates. Love forgives and love makes peace. Love is the reason we go on and the reason life is worth living.

Who We Are

It's true, we have our differences. But as a people, we share a common core. We are a culture of pioneers and refugees, survivors and builders. We are those who've come together in spite of our differences and built an oasis out of the once inhospitable landscape. Though we have often clashed and let our vices impede progress, the better angels of our nature continually strive upwards, guided by our virtues and ideals, to build a community of opportunity and prosperity for all.

We've come from hostility to build harmony. We've known pain and then found peace. We've known oppression and laboured for freedom. No goal is too large when our hearts are set on our shared goodwill. Despite our differences, we are a people of coming together to turn famine into flourishing and poverty into prosperity.

Part III
Metaphysics

Beginning of Metaphysics

Sometimes, the world falls from a state of good to a state of bad. And it becomes undeniable.

The mind is a raging current, and we can't stop its flow. Consciousness, the felt experience of existing, the quality of being alive (qualia), and all the other things we can't quite put in a box.... Where does this abyss lead? What is this all about at the end of the day?

I keep running from the something. Perhaps chasing or being chased, but I keep moving. I exist. I Think. I live in this world, and sometimes that isn't a pleasant experience.

Perhaps I'm chasing after an idea, trying to figure something out. Or maybe I'm chasing something in my mind, only to realize I am what's being chased. I realized what I thought was something other than me, is also something that's a part of me. I am a small part of something larger. The thing that makes me alive and exist is the same thing that makes reality possible. I am the seen and the seer becoming one. Knowledge and that which knowledge considers are part of the same larger whole. The knower and the known are one.

We are life itself. We are love. And we should treat others as love.

We should never speak to one another as enemies. We once spoke to each other trying to destroy rather than create life and love. We spread evil and hateful things rather than spreading that which is good, beneficial, and uplifting.

Let us become friends before we become enemies.

...

Love yourself. And love the world as you love yourself. This is it.

In this section, I'm going to try to talk about what reality is and then think about what we are in a spiritual and emotional sense. What is this world, and what are we? This chapter is different from the rest and has received mixed feedback depending on what you're interested in. So, buckle up, and or just move on to the next chapter at any point if it isn't your cup of tea.

...

We're individuals made of matter, but there's something about Me as a Self that is different from this matter I'm composed of. I am made of matter, but I am not just matter. What am I?

Am I the matter I'm made of, or am I the arrangement of the matter? What is this arrangement and how does it affect the matter? Whatever it is, it is always one step beyond the matter; it can't be put in the box.

All is one. But the seer sees the seen and then the one is separate, yet contained within the larger vessel. The seer and the seen exist in the same vessel, and this exists even if it stops existing in its original form.

Life pops into existence like a blooming flower. But even though the flower dies, that force behind the flower is eternal. The force of life and the feeling of existence is immortal.

What is Really Real?

Stop! Please don't think of a pink elephant!

Now, I bet you couldn't help but imagine a pink elephant. Hopefully you just pictured one in your mind rather than *hearing* and *smelling* a pink elephant—oh wait, you just imagined that too.

Although you experienced the pink elephant, it may seem obvious that the pink elephant doesn't actually exist.

But sometimes, it may seem hard to distinguish between our inward experience of reality and how reality really is. For example, when I show you this rectangle, you perceive it as white.

But what if I told you that this rectangle is actually black? Turns out, I just inverted the colours with a computer.

What is the real colour of the rectangle? And how would you have known the real colour of the rectangle based on just your perception? Does the rectangle even have a "real" colour?

Situations like these make us question the nature of human perception, experience, and reality itself.

Something I find interesting is the human brain under the influence of psychedelics. Psychedelics commonly cause hallucinations, which simply put, makes the user see, hear, or experience things that aren't really there.

But what is actually happening in the brain while someone is hallucinating on psychedelics?

There's a part of the human brain that is responsible for filtering our perceptions of the world. Let's call this part of the brain, 'Frank.' Frank the filter. The vast number of sounds, shapes, colours, and other sensory inputs happening all the time would be enough to drive someone crazy. So being the nice guy he is, Frank filters out a bunch of these sensory inputs so we can survive and function in the world without going totally insane.[118]

Now what's really fascinating is that when someone is under the influence of a psychedelic, this part of the brain shuts off. Frank takes a break and lets all these sensory inputs through, which causes the hallucinations and delusions people experience while on psychedelics. In other words, psychedelics reduce activity in brain regions responsible for filtering one's perception (as found by several studies, although it is still debated).[119]

What's the implication of this? Well, it seems to suggest that people hallucinating on psychedelics are experiencing reality for what it really is before these sensory inputs are filtered by the brain. In this case, are normal states of consciousness delusional if your perception of the world is heavily filtered from what it really is? How much of what you perceive to be real are just distortions and delusions?

There's an idea from the ancient Greek skeptics that suggests we can never know the world directly. All we can know about the world is what we perceive. Our understanding of reality is always viewed through our perception of it. This is an important distinction to make because there might be a difference between our perception of the world and the way the world is. And if there is a difference, how would we know?

One of the most famous ancient Greek philosophers is Plato. In his famous allegory of the cave, Plato compares our perception of reality to shadows cast onto a wall and suggests that the world we experience are the shadows rather than the things that casts the shadows.[120]

A similar idea is proposed by the German philosopher, Emmanuel Kant, who argues that we should distinguish between our experience of reality and reality itself. Kant says there's the Noumena, which is the world as it actually is. This is what exists. This is reality. Then there's the Phenomena, which is the world as we perceive it to be. Kant believed that humans can never perceive reality as it is because reality must always be viewed through the lens of our perception.[121] Much like how distant stars and galaxies can only be seen through a telescope, our experience of reality can only be seen through the lens of our perception. Essentially, we can't know what is real, only what we *perceive* as real.

Similar to the debated colour of the rectangle, how do we know that our perception of what is real is *really* real?

This idea is also reflected in an old Buddhist proverb that says, "Where there is perception, there is deception."[122] When we perceive reality, our perception of the world is often different from how the world really is.

This idea is demonstrated in the famous psychological experiment conducted at Harvard University called *The Gorilla Experiment*, also known as *The Invisible Gorilla*.[123] The researchers asked participants to watch a video of two teams of people wearing black and white shirts passing a basketball back and forth. The researchers asked participants to pay attention to the passes and keep track of how many times a basketball is thrown. After the video, researchers asked the participants how many passes they counted. Then to the surprise of the participants, the researchers asked, "But did you see the gorilla?" A whopping 50% of participants reported not seeing a gorilla in the video. Many were convinced there was no gorilla. Surely, they think, they would've seen it. Yet when they rewatch the video, a person in a gorilla suit clearly appears from one side of the screen and then stops in the middle of the crowd to beat their chest before proceeding to the other side of the screen. Most participants are shocked by the realization they had missed this obvious moment in the video. The gorilla was not a part of their reality.

Why was this? Why do most viewers not see the gorilla?

Researchers call this phenomenon "inattention blindness" and suggest we're less likely to perceive things we aren't looking for. When we're focussed on a task, most of our perception is directed toward that task. *The Gorilla Experiment* demonstrates that our attention is limited and that our perception of reality is often different from how reality really is.

It's almost as if our perception of the world is shaped by the lens through which we view it. It's almost as if the world creates itself through the lens we use to perceive it.

There's a story about a Buddhist monk and two women moving to a new town. The first woman asks the monk if she should move to this town, and the monk asks her, "What do you think of your current town?" She replies, "Oh it's horrible. The people are rude, it's boring, and there's lots I don't like about it." The monk says, "This town is much the same. Don't move here." The second woman asks the monk if she should move to this town. The monk asks her, "How do you like your current town?" She replies, "Oh it's lovely. The people are wonderful, it's beautiful, but I'm just looking for a change." The monk says to her, "This town is very much the same. I think you will like it here."

This story highlights the idea that your experience of the world is what you perceive it to be. In the story, was the town good or bad? It turns out that the same town can be both good and bad depending on the person perceiving it. And the more we try to understand what the world is apart from our perception of it, the more we realize the world independent from our experience is not as simple as we once thought.

In fact, the world is weird. Very weird. And when we try to understand reality through our modern scientific framework, it gets even weirder. The implications of quantum physics seem to suggest that reality works differently than we previously thought. Matter can act as a wave and a particle at the same time, particles seem to be in two places at once, and the very act of observing reality seems to change it.

The iconic experiment that exposed this strange behaviour of reality is called *The Double Slit Experiment*.[124] In this experiment, scientists fired particles through one of two slits and noticed an interference pattern on the surface where the particles landed. An interference pattern occurs when two waves merge together, causing the waves to be amplified in some sections and canceled out in others, making an image of parallel straight lines with spaces between them on the surface where the particles landed.

The crazy thing is that particles can only do this if they act as a wave and a particle at the same time. To have this wave-like effect, the particle must go through both slits at the same time, which seems absurd to our common sense. After all, there's only one particle. How can one particle travel through two slits at the same time? The most likely explanation is that the particle acts as a wave, traveling through both slits at once.

What's bizarre though is that observing the wave/particle seems to change how it acts. When scientists try to measure the wave and observe it traveling through both openings at the same time, it behaves like a particle travelling through only one slit. But when the particle is not being measured, it goes back to acting like a wave and travels through both slits at once. It appears that the act of observing reality actually changes how it behaves.

What does this say about the nature of reality? Before reality is observed, physicists say that a particle is in a state of superposition—which means reality could be in multiple positions at once. The particle could be in all-positions, hence the name super-position. But once the particle is observed and measured by an observer, the wave function collapses, and the particle is in just one position. This seems to suggest that our perception of the world is what influences reality, rather than reality influencing our perception.

The phenomena of superposition can have significant effects on the real world, as shown in the thought experiment of *Schrödinger's Cat*. *Schrödinger's Cat* is a thought experiment, sometimes described as a paradox, proposed by Austrian physicist Erwin Schrödinger in 1935. It illustrates the concept of superposition in quantum mechanics, which states that a particle can exist in multiple states at the same time. In this thought experiment, "A cat is locked in a steel box with a small amount of a radioactive substance such that after one hour there is an equal probability of one atom either decaying or not decaying. If the atom decays, a device smashes a vial of poisonous gas, killing the cat. However, until the box is opened and the atom's wave function collapses, the atom's wave function is in a superposition of two states: decay and non-decay. Thus, the cat is in a superposition of two states: alive and dead."[125] According to the principles of quantum mechanics, the cat is both alive and dead at the same time until the box is opened and the state of the cat is observed. This demonstrates the idea that the act of observation can influence the outcome of an event at the quantum level.

What is reality without us? Well, we can't say for certain, because we can't know what the world is apart from our perception of it. And our very perception of reality may play an active role in creating the world. So, what can we know for certain? What is really real?

A French philosopher tried to tackle this question and determine what we can know for sure. In his famous work, *Meditations*, Rene Descartes investigates what we can definitively know about reality. Descartes was skeptical about what we can know from our perception, theorizing that our senses could be just the product of hallucinations, or our brain in a vat being stimulated by electrical impulses, or even an evil demon deceiving us into believing a false view of reality. Descartes set out to determine what we can know for certain about reality and determined that all we can know for certain is that we exist. In his famous statement, "I think, therefore I am", Descartes suggests that although we can be skeptical of everything else, our own existence cannot be questioned.[126]

So, what's real? What is *really* real?

Your existence.

Your experience.

Your life.

Cherish it. Revel in it. Own it. It is yours and experienced by no one else.

Don't get hung up over stuff that doesn't matter and makes you feel weak, miserable, or exhausted. For all you know, these things that are getting you down might not even exist. They certainly aren't as they seem. All that is certain is how you feel. All you know that is really real is what you're experiencing right now, every moment, of every day, of every week, of every year.

At the end of your years, on your deathbed, you'll realize that your life was the sum total of your experiences and how you perceived the world. And you'll ask yourself, "Am I happy with the world I created?" Because that is your reality. That is what's really real.

Aristotle and Infinity: The Force of God

Aristotle offers a famous argument that has been used to justify the existence of God. This argument is often called "The Unmoved Mover" and goes as follows:

Everything we observe that is in motion was put in motion by something else. If we work backward and follow the series of motion and movements, either this regress will go into infinity, or we will arrive at a force/object that set everything into motion that itself was unmoved.[127]

Aristotle argues that there cannot be an infinite regress of motion or "moved movers." Instead, he argues that the logical answer is that there must be an unmoved mover to set the cosmos into motion.

This unmoved mover has been understood by religious thinkers as God.

But why is it that there cannot be an infinite series of movements going back forever? Of course, we know our universe had a beginning marked by the Big Bang.[128] We can trace the series of motion in our universe back to its creation, but what about before that? We also know that matter can't be created nor destroyed, and that all the matter in the universe was present at the Big Bang. So, what happened before the Big Bang? Matter was there; it always existed. Could there have been movement happening before the formation of our universe? Perhaps this motion was in another universe that eventually collapsed in on itself, which then expanded outwards to form another universe during the Big Bang. Is it unreasonable to think this process has been happening for eternity?[129]

If this is the case that matter and motion have been around *forever*, then there can be an infinite series of motions or "moved movers." Some people might think this challenges the religious idea of God, but I don't think it does.

If there is a force of motion that has been around *literally forever* and is responsible for the motion of *the entire cosmos*, doesn't this also sound like God? Perhaps infinity itself as an object is the unmoved mover.

Why Does Stuff Move?

What forces govern the movement of the world? There seems to be movement in the physical universe and movement in our experiential world, but what started it?

The moving principle of the forces/patterns that govern the physical world are metaphysically the same things as the forces/patterns that govern consciousness, thought of as experiential movement.

What is the source of this movement? Where does movement come from? Movement, especially movement of the mind, seems patterned, expressing fractals and archetypes. Experience *experiences* this movement. Consciousness lives in the world and perceives these patterns all around itself.

Experience *experiences* conscious existence and symbolically represents the world, trying to understand reality. The Self tries to explain to itself (and other selves) what the world is and how it works. The Self tries to articulate patterns and does so through symbols, metaphor, and myth. This is the power of story and the experience of a narrative.

These stories and narratives appear to have similarities and seem to be based on an ultimate or meta-narrative. The True Narrative, that which all the other narratives are based, is the narrative structure of Experience itself. It tries to show the patterns, which are often expressed as mythologies.

What is the final aim of this experience? What is the nature of Experience? Why did organic life become embedded with the ability to experience at all? What is Experience trying to do if it *experiences* anything? Why did Experience emerge? Experience is perceiving patterns and expression patterns. But what is the source of these patterns? What's this pattern that governs the rules of the cosmos? What is the source of the movement of our world? Both the movement of the external universe and the movement of our consciousness, where does this movement come from? What is this Moving Principle?

Materialism is Demonstrably False

What force keeps the world functioning? What structure binds particles together? Why do particles bind together, and where does that thing come from? Some of these answers are just basic facts of reality that we have to accept.

These facts of the world are articulated by physics and our conception of fundamental forces. These forces are very real and are very *non-material*. Our material universe is governed by non-material laws. And these laws of the universe that govern the material world exist independently of the material world. This is a genuine problem for materialism and for those who believe that the universe can be entirely explained by its material components.

There's something more out there beyond the matter of the universe. This is not an assumption, but a conclusion.

Since these non-material laws that govern the material universe exist, they can only exist beyond the material universe. There must be a level of reality literally beyond our material landscape. This is undeniable given the existence of the laws of physics and mathematics.

This leaves the door open for physicalism (the belief the universe can be fully explained by the physical forces of nature), but it slams the door on materialism. It exposes that physicalism is just a religion. To be more specific, physicalism is the scientific container for eternal truths of reality and the Divine.

Physics comes from the Greek word 'physica', meaning 'study of nature.'[130] In a modern phrase, physics studies the true nature of reality. Physics explains how the forces of nature control the entire universe. Reality can be divided into two distinct categories. On the one hand, there's the universe governed by forces, and then on the other hand, there's the forces themselves. These exist in two different worlds.

How is this anything close to materialism?

Was The Universe Created?

In the beginning, there was nothing.

But true nothingness is impossible. Nothingness will always have the Potential to be something. True nothingness, the lack of all things, would have to be absent of Potential. But Potential is the necessary by-product of nothing. Nothingness and Potential must exist together. Nothing and Potential go hand in hand. The necessary existence of Potential then negates "no-thing" and leaves only Potential.

Some folks will argue that Potential is not a thing because it is non-material. These are the materialists. Materialism is the belief that all of reality can be reduced to its material components. Since Potential is not a material object, materialists say that Potential doesn't exist. But Potential surely exists even though it is non-material. Plus, we act as if Potential exists all the time. We even know that Potential exists as a scientific fact, which is how we can accurately and repeatedly predict the behaviour of the material world. This Potential is where we base the laws of physics and the fundamentals of reality.

Consider this quick example. Hydrogen and Oxygen have the Potential to form water. They will never form BBQ sauce. The Potential for Hydrogen and Oxygen to become water is real, although prior to its formation, this reality is non-material. If we define material existence as the criteria for reality, then we're doing ourselves a disservice in our pursuit of the Truth.

Let's get back to nothingness.

If we start with nothing, then we have only Potential, since the Potential to be something is the necessary result of nothing.

This is the void. Chaos. Chaos means disorder and confusion. Chaos is the formless mess of all that could be. The chaos of the void is both nothing and everything all at once. It is pure Potential.

Then came Gaia from nothing—with nothing—necessarily.

Gaia is the first being of the ancient Greek creation myth and emerges from Chaos.[131] Greek mythology associates Gaia with fertility, and the force of creation itself. Fertility is Potential. The Potential for things to be created. Potential is that which can be. This is the force behind creation. For anything to be created, there must be Potential. When starting with nothing, there can only be potential. When starting with nothing, Potential is necessary and cannot be avoided. This is symbolically represented by Gaia (the force of Potential and creation) coming into being from the void. Her existence is necessitated through nothingness, just as Potential is embedded in nothing.

Everything that could be must follow a blueprint. It doesn't *just happen*. Things happen according to rules. There must be a pre-existing order for things to follow. Chaos has the Potential to become something according to an order. This order may not be a tangible reality, but the rules and structure of this order exist prior to the material manifestation. This is the way things must happen so that they logically and causally make sense. Everything that happens in the physical world only happens in accordance with what *can* happen. It's as if there is a pre-existing structure to reality—a cosmic blueprint for the way things work.

This is the Potential. This underlying structure of reality is the foundation on which all things are built. This structure is the tracks on which the material world must follow. This is the way things must be and they cannot be other than how they are. This structure, Potential, is the rules that reality follows. This structure is the Word by which the physical world emerges from chaos. These possibilities of happenings are like railroad tracks the material world must follow. Just as a train can only travel on train tracks, the material universe can only behave according to what is possible. Things cannot happen other than how they are able to. In a way, Potential exists as true before these things actually come to be. The necessity of causality and order exists as Potential, which is independent of the material world. The material world relies on this Potential and structural order to operate.

So, how does stuff just happen then? How does creation and the universe come from pure Potential? How does something come from nothing or from just Potential?

All we know with a high degree of certainty is that:
1. If we start with nothing, we necessarily have Potential.
2. Potential is not nothing, so we can't actually have pure nothingness.
3. Potential is necessary for the universe to function.

The big question is: how do we go from just non-material Potential to the material universe?

Although the genesis of the material universe may seem too overwhelming and daunting of a task to comprehend, we know it had to happen. Look around. If there was a point in time before a material universe, it somehow came to be. If there was a time when there was only nothing and Potential, then surely the material universe had to come from nothing/Potential. But how? How do we go from just non-material Potential to the material universe?

The answer: we don't have to go from a non-material Potential to a material universe. Perhaps the universe doesn't need a beginning. The material universe could have always existed. Our universe had a "beginning," but the materials that makes up our universe could have existed for eternity. If we are being honest with ourselves, we don't know what matter was doing before the Big Bang and the rapid expansion of our universe.

Perhaps we've been asking the wrong questions. Rather than asking "How did the universe begin?" We should ask, "Did the universe begin?"

Matter exists. This is a fact that we can observe. And according to the work of Antoine Lavoisier, matter cannot be created or destroyed.[132] If matter cannot be created or destroyed, then, it has always been. So, it could very well be the case that matter has always been embodying the structure and order of Potential.

There is no need to understand how Potential gives rise to creation or the material universe, because "creation" has always existed, just like Potential has always existed. "Creation" may have never been created but instead could have always been, *forever*. Both the material and the underlying order by which the material operates could be eternal. While it is true that mere Potential does not necessitate the material universe, it seems likely that the matter of the universe has always been here.

So what happened before the Big Bang? What happened before our universe exploded from a singularity, that infinitely small point when all point where all the matter of the universe was condensed?

Well, there had to be something before the Big Bang. Otherwise, the universe was *always* a singularity *forever*, and then randomly exploded at an arbitrary moment. Alternatively, the matter of the material universe could have been doing something else before the Big Bang and the singularity that came before it. This could suggest that the matter of our current universe was once something larger than a singularity before it was a singularity. Or it was always a singularity and then the expansion of our universe randomly happened… But this randomness is absurd and negates the causality of the material universe. This randomness contradicts all of physics for something to just "happen." Why? Why did it happen? Why then and not another time? By the laws of causality, there must have been a reason. Unless we're accepting that non-causal randomness genuinely happens on the cosmic scale which is a huge problem for the deterministic model of reality. This defies all logical and causal possibilities.

Or we can speculate that the expansion of our universe wasn't random, and the universe itself *chose* to rapidly expand. This means the universe as a whole is capable of actually choosing something and means it might have some form of cosmic consciousness.

Both these implications for a random expansion of our material universe seem absurd, and at the very least, debatable. The most reasonable answer is that matter has always been here, and the materials of our universe existed before the singularity that rapidly expanded our universe. However, it seems impossible (or at least extremely difficult) to speculate what the material universe was doing before the Big Bang.

Since matter is eternal, then so is the order that underlies it. The order of the universe and its Potential is eternal. It is "God", for lack of a better word. Or perhaps more accurately, God is a symbolic representation of this cosmic order and Potential. Perhaps God is the best way to describe something so infinite and beyond our comprehension that underlies the fundamentals of reality.

These ideas are not intended to provide a literal account of creation, but rather to offer a conceptual framework to understand how we arrived at where we are right now. By understanding what the basic building blocks of creation are *in theory*, we can understand why the material universe couldn't have come from nothing, and that true nothingness is impossible.

Through considering the concepts of Nothing, Potential, and the properties of matter, we can consider a material reality prior to the Big Bang and the "creation" of our universe. When we combine this understanding with the way we know how the world works right now, we get a fuller understanding of why things are at all, how they came to be, and most importantly, why that makes sense. Basically, we get to the conclusion that the universe has always existed. Or at least, whatever the universe is contained in has always existed. The state of being beyond the universe is sometimes called "cosmos." Asking "how was the cosmos created?" is an invalid question because it implies the cosmos *must* have had an origin. A better question is removing "how" and asking, "was the cosmos created?" To which the answer seems to be "no."

...

That's all fine and dandy, but how does Consciousness come to be? And that's the question. We can talk all day about matter and the origin of the universe, but how did this matter "wake up?"

It seems that since matter operates according to non-material eternal principles, eventually through the process of evolution by natural selection, matter becomes so complex that the non-material eternal order "bleeds through" to the material universe. The material world emulates the eternal world to such a high degree of complexity that the perceptions and information processing of life become aware of itself, its existence, and its own mortality. Consciousness is a being's awareness of its participation in the patterns of the cosmos. Something that is capable of perception and continues to evolve and enhance its perceptual capacity will eventually perceive the world to such a high degree of effectiveness that it becomes aware of itself. Becoming aware of itself allows a being to become a Self. Once this happens, it is one of the most complex things to ever exist. Its awareness allows it the capacity to reflect on itself and its own embodiments of the patterns of creation, its embodiment of the structure and rules of the physical world, and its own embodiment of the eternal principles of reality. Consciousness recognizes itself in the grand narrative of how the world works, and the structure of reality unfolding before us.

The implications of this are that You are the universe experiencing itself. Your consciousness is the eternal truth peaking in on itself and realizing what it is. The underlying structure and order of conscious experience exists outside of time and space, outside of the material universe, but provides the blueprint for which matter is able to arrange itself in such a way as to become *aware* of what it is. How this happens is a question I'm not qualified to address. But regardless of how conscious experience and reality comes to be, You are It.

Patterns and Fractals

This universe and everything in it are bound by the laws and limitations of possibility. Scientific laws, mathematical truths, and physical possibility constrain all things. Due to these constraints of the natural world, nature unfolds in patterns. Growth, death, multiplication, and decay; nature can only play out in so many ways.

As a human being, you're a part of nature. You display various patterns in your life. Although it may feel as though the infinite choices before you allow you to do anything, this "anything" is always broken down into larger themes and categories. Creation, anger, love, community, adventure, exploration, leadership, rebellion, and striving for belonging, just to name a few, are all examples of distinct themes that govern our actions. There are a finite number of these themes that govern our behaviour. Our life unfolds according to these patterns.

As human beings, we also exist in social networks and communities. The interactions of these social groups are also constrained by patterns. Much like your individual behaviour is constrained by distinct themes, so is the behaviour of social groups. These social groups, also being a part of nature, unfold in the same patterns of the natural world.

What's fascinating is the existence of behavioural patterns at different levels of observation. The patterns of the natural world exist as fractals. Fractals are self-similar patterns that persist throughout an entire structure. This triangular structure is an example of a fractal in how the same pattern exists throughout all levels of the whole.

Figure 6: Image by Beojan Stanislaus, changed to black-and-white. To view the original image, visit https://commons.wikimedia.org/wiki/File:Sierpinski_triangle.svg

Notice how the same triangular pattern repeats itself to infinity. If you were to zoom into this shape, you would see the same pattern continue.

Fractals don't just occur in mathematical structures, but in nature as well. The fern leaf is a perfect example of fractals in nature.

Figure 7: Image by Laug, changed to black-and-white. To view the original image, visit https://commons.wikimedia.org/wiki/File:Barnsley_fern _2000x2000.png

Each individual fern leaf resembles the whole. If you were to isolate just one fern leaf and zoom in on its smaller leaves, it would look just like the whole fern leaf. It seems obvious that nature exists in fractals and patterns. But human beings seem to exist according to fractals and patterns as well.

Consider our planet. When observing the Earth both in the present and throughout its history, human social groups have had conflict since the beginning of time. From a global perspective, conflict is a pattern displayed by the human species, in some cases engulfing entire continents in war. And if we zoom into one country, we can find conflict in the form of civil wars or political tension. Further, if we continue to zoom into a city, we can still find conflict in the form of regional politics or gang violence. Although the scope of our investigation changes, the pattern of conflict remains.

The same is true for other patterns of human behaviour. Love, cooperation, trade, openness, hatred, oppression, betrayal, and other distinct themes of human behaviour are observable from the relationships between countries down to the interactions between individuals. From different heights, the same pattern is present. Human behaviour unfolds according to these patterns and fractals. In some sense, the patterns that underly human behaviour are more real than humans themselves, since the patterns that humans act out go beyond the individual humans who express them.

A unique feature of human beings is that we tell stories. Stories also express these universal patterns and fractals. There are only so many stories we can tell until they become repetitive. They fit into a finite number of categories: adventure, romance, mystery, drama, action, etc. But when you break down the thousands of stories in a genre, we notice that they're often the same story being told. These stories have the same characters, same archetypes, same plot, and same problems.

Even emotions are governed by these patterns and fractals. Consider anger, love, boredom, desire, sadness, excitement, and the rest of the emotions that possess our consciousness. We only have a certain number of emotions that we can feel. There are only so many patterns the universe allows for consciousness to experience. Experience itself and consciousness seem to be an expression of these patterns. Reality seems to dance with itself as it changes and unfolds into infinity. Reality is like a cosmic symphony of music in an ordered harmony. And this harmony has notes that all sing of patterns and fractals.

It's important to consider the implications of these patterns for our lives. Some of these patterns are better than others for achieving a desirable life of prosperity and fulfillment. You're condemned to express a pattern, but you can choose what this pattern is. It's crucial that we recognize what patterns there are to act out, and then identify which pattern we act acting out. The next step is to think about what pattern we want to start acting out if we aren't acting it out already. Perhaps the pattern we are currently embodying is no good and undesirable. Maybe we're lazy, unmotivated, angry, etc. Not choosing a pattern to embody is also a pattern itself. Refusal to play a character doesn't change the fact you're still playing a character. That's just the character you chose to play.

We don't have a choice but to play a character. Nonetheless, we get to choose which character we want to play.

The One and The Many: Unity and Multiplicity

Things start simple, then become complex. Complexity grows out of the simplicity as a natural process. From The One, multiplicity emerges. From The One, The Many springs forth. A unity fractures into multiplicity. And from that multiplicity, another unity will form once more. This pattern unfolds in a fractal-like manner, from lenses great and small. The One and The Many play out their drama with the world as their stage.

History is the canvas to view the patterns of life unfold. Consciousness, or more accurately put, the unconscious patterns we act out as a social species, unfold across time. When we zoom out our focus from the individual person, we notice our individual identity is overshadowed by our membership in the human species. Although we are individuals with a Self, aspirations, and desires, we are vessels for human patterns to unfold.

The tribe once united, fractures to infighting. A collection of people will begin harmoniously and then separate to the drama of human affairs. New tribes form out of the division, restarting the process.

A land of multiple spiritual faiths eventually becomes dominated by one shared religion. From the one religion, it will fracture into various denominations. And from these denominations, they will further separate until a new unity emerges from the chaos of multiplicity.

The land controlled by warlords, bandits, and mercenaries will skirmish until they united under one political unit. This unit will then fragment into new groups that will war with each other, eventually forming a new unity in the future.

A nation great and powerful will crumble under the weight of its unity. One country will either be absorbed into another political unit, or will divide amongst itself internally, giving birth to new nations from the corpse of the original.

A market will have many vendors, all selling items for customers to purchase. As the market plays out, vendors will merge together. Some will become successful on their own, driving their competition out of business. The market once composed of many vendors will have become dominated by a few united monopolies. Eventually, the monopolies will collapse, either by bankruptcy, antitrust division, or closure. Then the market will be without domineering monopolies and will be open to smaller vendors and sellers, restarting the economic process.

These patterns aren't just unique to humans. All the natural world behaves according to rules, patterns, and possibilities sewn into the fabric of reality. From the forests of Earth to the farthest corners of the universe, patterns guide the movement of this world.

From a unity, a multiplicity will emerge. The One will fracture into The Many. The chaos of The Many will transform into a unity. This is a pattern older than time itself.

A decaying heap of matter will be the foundation of future life. Plants will emerge, and a mighty tree will grow. Over time, the tree will wither or collapse. And eventually the dead tree will decay, returning to the Earth, becoming the fertilizer for future growth and multiplicity.

Our universe is said to have come from the Big Bang—an explosion of matter and energy that was condensed into a singular point in space and time. This One gave birth to The Many as the cosmos unfolded. From the chaos of this multiplicity, matter collected into larger unities, creating stars and planets. These stars and planets were then lost among the trillions of planetary bodies which then formed into the larger unities of solar systems and galaxies.

If you are among The Many, lost in the thrashing ocean of chaos, know that the current multiplicity will eventually become The One. And if you currently sit secure in an undivided unity, The One, know that it will fracture and become The Many, continuing the eternal dance.

Observing these patterns illuminates the nature of reality to be organic and ever-changing. The world around us is the stage for an eternal dance between The One and The Many.

Possibility

Things cannot happen other than how they can happen. Why is this? Why are some things possible and other things are not? Why is Possibility the way it is? What constrains what is possible and what is not?

Possibility itself is fixed. The Possibility of the material universe and the constraints on the behaviour of matter are as real as the material things themselves, though this Possibility is non-material.

Possibility itself is a thing that exists.

Consider the triangle. Why does a triangle have three sides? Can a triangle have any number of sides other than three? No. Why not? Even if the truth of a three-sided triangle is in reference to a material triangle, the *impossibility* of a triangle having anything other than three sides is immaterial. Why does the material triangle manifest this way? It's a logical impossibility for a shape with internal angles equaling 180 degrees to have anything other than three sides. The mathematical Possibility constraining a triangle is distinct from the matter of a triangle.

Possibility itself is a distinct type of non-material existence. Even in a state of nothingness, fundamental truths still exist; one plus one still equals two.

Possibility is what governs the material. What is Possible constrains the interaction of matter throughout the material universe. Possibility is the mechanisms by which the material universe is bound. The underlying structure of what's possible for the material world is fundamental to reality, yet essentially non-material.

Reality cannot behave other than how it is able to. This Possibility is non-material.

Metaphysics: Matter, Motion, and Mechanics

Why study metaphysics? Honestly, who cares?

Well, you should care if you want what's best for you. Understanding metaphysics and how the world works is like understanding the programming of a video game. When you understand the constraints and possibilities of a game, you'll know how to thrive in the game. And who doesn't want to thrive? Much like a sports game, if you understand the rules, then you can develop a strategy. And with a strategy, you'll have a path to victory.

Metaphysics is the investigation into the workings of reality. The word comes from the Greek term "beyond physics" and seeks to understand the fundamental nature of existence.[133] Sure, the laws of physics tell us about how the physical world works, things like gravity, electricity, motion, and stuff like that, but what causes these forces to exist? What lies beyond the forces of physics? What sits underneath the world and holds it together, allowing for the harmony of the cosmos to unfold before our eyes? Why does it work the way it does?

If we can answer these questions, we'll have insight into the innermost workings of reality. As beings who live in reality, understanding how reality works will be beneficial to us. If we wish to avoid pitfalls and suffering, it's best we know how they're created. If we seek wealth, wellbeing, or love, it's helpful to know where these things originate. All things stem from reality—triumph and tribulations, prosperity and poverty, light and darkness. If we understand how reality works, then we'll know how everything in reality originates. And if we know how everything originates, we can become the originators. We can use this knowledge to become the creators of our own experience.

Consider this a study of applied metaphysics.

So where do we begin?

We begin with experience.

Reality will always be understood through our experience of it. There can be no other way. Our experience might be false or misguided, causing one to believe things that aren't really the case. But what alternative do we have? Can we understand reality outside of our conscious experience of it? It doesn't seem so. Even pure logic, rationality, or divine revelation of truth is still perceived through our experience. Our experience is our reality and there's no way around it.

Something immediate to our experience of the word is matter. There's this stuff literally everywhere. And it seems like we can touch it, move it, and interact with it. We can even manipulate it and change it. When we look at ourselves, we realize that we are also composed of this matter. According to our experience, matter seems to be a basic building block of reality.

Some say matter is *the* building block of reality. Materialists say everything is matter. This doctrine of materialism argues that everything is reducible to matter and can be explained by its materials. And they make a compelling case. By understanding reality as fundamentally material, we have been able to discover the laws of physics and accurately predict how the universe will behave. Once materialism arose on the scene, the world was no longer explained by random events or the arbitrary will of the gods. The world became consistent, predictable, and most importantly, rationally understandable once we learned how matter behaves.

But there's one glaring hole unaccounted for by the materialist worldview…

Motion.

Matter moves and we don't know why.

Everything in motion is set in motion by something else. But nothing is the cause of its own motion. Something moving is moved by something else, and that thing was also moving. Where did this movement come from? It seems movement can be traced back to the beginning of the universe and the initial explosion of the Big Bang. But what movement set the Big Bang in motion?

When something is in motion, the motion seems to transcend the thing itself. The movement of matter goes beyond the matter. In some sense, the material world is lifeless atoms that are moved around by motion. This motion is like an unending current moving between different material vessels. Motion is like a torch being passed along by all physical things that move. Physical things themselves do not move but are moved by motion.

Some might say that matter does move itself. Matter is constantly in motion. Even when an object is at rest, the individual atoms in the object are constantly vibrating. Although this is technically movement, this movement seems different from the motion that moves objects through space. The subtle vibration of atoms is distinctly different from the motion of a ball being kicked through the air, dominos moving one another, or the movement that explodes a star. Although matter may vibrate, this is different from motion as we generally think of it.

But this constant vibration of matter is interesting. Even when an atom is not being acted on by something else, it will always be vibrating. Is the atom causing its own vibration? Or is the atom being vibrated by something else?

The Tibetan Buddhists believe that Motion is the fundamental reality. They have an idea that "the world *is* movement."[134] They're convinced that there are no objects "in movement," but that movement is the fundamental nature of the world. Perhaps they're onto something since all matter can't help but be in constant vibration. But does this mean that matter *is* motion?

It doesn't seem so. According to our experience in the world, matter appears to exist independent of motion. Although matter may be constantly in motion, there seems to be a stark difference between the two.

If matter cannot create its own motion, then where does motion come from? Perhaps the Tibetan Buddhists were right in thinking of motion as something fundamental to the universe.

Imagine all of the matter in the universe as a large blanket spread out flat on the ground. When you see a blanket move, it seems like the movement is coming from something moving under the blanket. Think of what it would look like for a small animal to be running around underneath the blanket causing a mound in the blanket to move throughout. Just like the material universe, we only see the one side of the blanket being moved. Surely, the blanket doesn't move itself. The movement comes from something else that moves the material blanket. If the universe is this blanket, there's a side underneath the material that we must delve into if we are to understand the true nature of reality. Underneath the blanket is not just motion, but the mechanisms and rules underlying the relationship between matter and motion.

On the other side of this blanket is the underside of reality. It's not material in the sense of being tangible or made of matter. Although it is not made of matter, it makes the matter behave as it does. The movement of the matter is housed between the materials of reality and its mechanisms. Like checking under the hood of a car, the underside of reality is what makes the whole vehicle function.

How do we conceptualize this underside?

Apart from matter, there's motion. Both exist distinctly from one another. But there's a third piece to this puzzle. Why does matter act as it does? There are certain things that matter can do, and certain things matter can't do. Some things are impossible while other things are possible. Why is this? What forces regulate matter? Why are the laws of physics the way they are? As far as we know, there are 26 universal constants that are eternal unchanging principles that govern the material world.[135] These constants (such as gravity and the speed of light) were not created, but discovered. Where do they come from? Moreover, why do things make sense at all? Just like motion exists separate from matter, *Possibility* exists separate from matter and motion. Logical, mathematical, and physical laws outline what is possible for the universe. These are a glimpse into the mechanisms of reality.

These mechanisms are real but not material. No one would dispute that one plus one is two. Yet it isn't a material thing that exists in the world. But it's true. No doubt, the logic of one plus one being two is real. There's a whole type of existence of things that are very real but very non-material. Matter and material things in the universe can be used to demonstrate these abstract truths, but the abstract truths are different than the material things. In fact, these non-material truths seem to underlie the material things, defining what's possible and impossible for the behaviour of matter.

Matter is like a train, and it can only travel where there's a track. Matter cannot do what is impossible for it to do. What is possible and impossible are the tracks laid for the matter to travel. The mechanisms of reality lay the tracks for where the matter can travel. The speed of light, types of elements, laws of thermodynamics, and the forces of electromagnetism, even logical axioms themselves, among other things, are what underlie all reality. The matter of our universe is constrained by these mechanics. The mechanics of reality are the programming of the cosmos. It is the code that all things operate according to. It is the ordering principle that governs all that exists. It is Possibility itself.

These three distinct things work together to form all of reality. Matter, Motion, and Mechanics are the three different things that exist.

...

None of this would be complete without considering where consciousness fits into this framework. That is what you are, fellow conscious being. What's cool about consciousness is that you are a part of reality while being able to realize your separateness from it. You are a distinct thing that is acted on by the world. While reality acts on you, you can also act on reality.

Where does consciousness fit into this framework? Consciousness is a special combination of these fundamental building blocks. Much like the laws of physics are a combination of matter and mechanics, consciousness emerges from a combination as well.

Consciousness is motion, but it isn't motion itself. It's indisputable that consciousness is something that moves. Our consciousness is called a train of thought for a reason. The mind is always in motion. Our consciousness moves so much that it can often be overwhelming. In fact, this is what yoga and meditation practices try to accomplish. Silencing this rapidly moving thing we call consciousness or mind is the goal of meditation so we can attain a state of being characterized by peace, calm, and tranquility (known as nirvana in Eastern traditions).

Consciousness is moving, but it isn't movement itself. What is being moved? It seems there's a difference between the movement of consciousness and movement in general. Consciousness seems to be the mechanics themselves in motion.

What we are is a culmination of the laws of nature. Our consciousness originates from the cosmos and is constrained by the possibility that underlies all of nature. The unique movement and flow of consciousness could happen when the cosmic mechanics themselves are in motion. It has been said that "you are the universe aware of itself."[136] Perhaps when the fundamental motion of reality is applied to the mechanisms that underlie the cosmos, consciousness is the result. Perhaps when these mechanisms in motion are housed in a material brain, this is when a Self or embodied Being emerges.

As I said before, I'm just a person with an opinion so take this however you want. What do I know? But I suspect there's value in seeing the world this way.

So, what good is this? You've made it this far and are rightfully asking what any of this information can do for us. Aside from the fun of thinking about the nature of reality (I know, I'm weird), knowing the nature of reality has practical results.

One thing we have to accept is that there will always be motion. Similar to the revelation of the Buddha under the Bodhi tree, everything is always changing. Movement will come, and motion touches all. This is especially true for social structures and for our lives. As conscious beings, our existence is defined by movement. The social structures and political circumstances created by conscious beings are also affected by motion.

Change is eternal. Motion is change. We must accept that both our lives and the social structures we inhabit will change over time. Since change is inevitable, it is futile to cling to sameness. Motion will come and we must barter with the change it brings. The world is an ocean with waves of motion and change. Rather than desperately clinging to our version of how the world should be and thrashing against the waves, more fulfillment will be had through riding the waves. Harness motion to your benefit and don't fight the eventual movement and change of all things.

Though change is eternal, some things don't change. For example, leaders and governments will always change, but the inevitability of authority is eternal. There will always be a leader although those in power will change over time. Wars will come and go, but conflict is inevitable. These examples are not exhaustive but highlight that there are some things that will always be.

The mechanics don't just apply to matter, but to all things of the cosmos, including the affairs of human beings. The mechanics of reality are timeless and unchanging. The speed of light is unchanging. The laws of physics are fixed (and even if they did change, whatever force caused them to change is a deeper and more fundamental force that governs the cosmos). Logical and mathematical truths will always be as they are. And human beings will be subject to the virtues and vices of human nature. Humans as social animals will be constrained by human psychology, motivations, and fears, just as mathematics is constrained by logic.

Built into the mechanics of human society are the possibilities for poverty and prosperity. Both have been with our species since the beginning of human civilization. Certain behaviours are conducive to prosperity and fulfillment, while certain behaviours condemn us to failure and misery. I've noticed that an attitude of spreading love, being a light to illuminate darkness, truthfulness, resisting whining and complaining, being diligent and hardworking, and striving to bring good into the world seem like behaviours conducive to prosperity, success, fulfillment, and human flourishing.

Open your eyes, look around, and listen to the world. Take note of what works and what doesn't. See what has brought good things for some folks and what has led others to misery. The world isn't purely random. Some behaviours are more conducive to prosperity than others. You can choose to embody these behaviours. Notice these patterns and the world will be in the palm of your hand. The good things of life can be yours if you know how to bring them about. Learn the mechanisms of human society and you will be a creator.

Existence, Separation, and Anxiety

That constant chatter behind our eyes. That busyness of the brain that simply won't turn off. Inquiry turns into interrogation. Thought becomes fraught. Dwelling, doubting, endless questioning and criticizing. So often we're being stressed out and being worried rather than just being. We fall from bliss into a world just not good enough. There's always a problem. Our mind is never content, never satisfied with the way things are, always scheming for improvement and progress. Leave this far-off world to which we go in our minds and return to the world of the here and now.

Anxiety is a retreat into the mind, that chaotic and majestic abyss. The cure to anxiety is not to think more of lessening it. Thinking anything about anxiety only makes the anxiety much worse. Thinking about anxiety, or any thought at all from our rational and intellectual ego pulls the rug out from under us. We fall from the physical world into a realm of ideas and archetypes.

To return to the light of day and climb from the crevices we've dug ourselves into, we must become one with ourselves and embrace our participation in the natural world of the human animal, ascending from the chaos of consciousness, that cyclical cynicism, that critical commentary, that Awareness which springs up from the dead matter and realizes it is all alone.

Of course, to say, "we must become one with ourselves" is to deprive the human being of their very choice and attitude of existence. The fundamental consciousness of one's being can choose to reject a path to the light, leading to some minds choosing to live in darkness. They get so caught up in the existence of darkness that they forget they stand in their own shadow. Perhaps they've been separated from the luminous Transcendence of Being long enough that their eyes would have trouble adjusting to its light. They've been in darkness so long they think the night is inevitable. The suffering of life and the painful misery of our existence cannot be cured, they say. If only they were to focus on just being rather than being pathologically thoughtful, then they would melt back into the world from which they were separated.

This is not to dissolve into God, but to dissolve into the core of what you are. It is the ultimate defiance against God, that oppressive force of externality. The void would be gone, and we would experience the blissful, essential, and harmonic transcendence that underlies material reality. Only then do we realize that the Divine is within us and that the God we project onto the world is centered in consciousness.

Immortality: The God Within and The God Without

I am immortal. I will never cease to exist. Although my body will die, I will not die. Because the thing inside me able to say "I" is built into the fabric of reality.

I am godly. I am divine. I am an immortal soul.

The Self is Divine. The differences between the core of ourselves and God is an illusion.

When I say, "I am God." I do not mean that I am God above anyone else. I am not God in an exclusive sense. Rather, anyone able to say and comprehend "I," is God. The ability to be an "I," is Divine, specifically because awareness and consciousness are transcendent.

There's divinity in the Self. Consciousness is the spark of the Divine. Awareness is sewn into the fabric of reality. Our selfhood is built into the structure of the cosmos; immortal, eternal, and transcending this specific incarnation. Within ourselves can the Infinite be found. Only then do we realize our connection to everything outside ourselves. The inside and the outside are One.

Immortality is not attained—it is realized.

We are immortal souls in a dying body. Our memories are attached to our body, not our consciousness. When our body dies, so do our memories. But awareness is left. This is what transcends and is housed in a new vessel, according to advocates of reincarnation. If this is true, then that which makes you, you, is the same thing at the core of everyone else. You are everyone else. We are all One, stemming from the same life force.

But perhaps I am wrong. Perhaps I am not God. I certainly don't feel like God. I think there is something divine about consciousness and awareness. But this doesn't necessarily make it godly or being God. Consciousness is divine.

Consciousness is part of the eternal and timeless structure of the cosmos. This is part of God, but not God itself. I am not all-knowing. I am not all-powerful. But I am Divine. I am Transcendent.

Perhaps there is the god within and the god without. The god within is consciousness and awareness. This is the deepest sense of our being that transcends this world. And the god without is the underlying structure of everything. Of course, the god within and the god without stem from the same underlying rules and mechanics of reality. This is what I consider to be God. I am an embodiment of this underlying structure, but I am not the structure itself. We can experience God, but we are not God. We are transcendent, sure. We are divine, sure. But we are not the ultimate reality.

Unless we are.... how do we know that we are not?

The structure of the cosmos is within us. We are God in the sense that we are the structure of reality. We are It. Our limitations come from our bodily form. Our ego. But once we strip away the limitations of our frail bodies and the mental frameworks of our identity, all we are left with is the eternal and timeless structure of awareness sewn into the fabric of reality. We are vessels of the divine. We are temples that house the gods. We are Transcendent.

Did I set the corners of the Earth? Did I fill the oceans?
No. I did no such thing. But I am an embodiment of that which did.

I may be the matter and the motion, but I am not the mechanics. I am an expression of the mechanics, a window into the transcendent core of reality. I am not the Thing itself. I am not the All. I am an expression of the All. But doesn't that make me the All? Does being made in God's image make one a god? Within me is a cosmic harmony, an orchestra where I am the music but not the conductor. Who is the conductor? The mechanisms that make me, are not me. They transcend me, but I am a part of them. So is it more accurate to say that within me is the Divine? I am divine to my core. But the Divine in its totality is not me in my limitation.

I do not blow the winds. I do not shine the stars or move the planets. But that which does all these things is the cause for my existence as well.

All things have a unity and stem from the same Transcendent core of the cosmos. This core is God. I am not God, but God is in me. You are not God, but God is in you. We are not God, but the ultimate and Transcendent reality shines through us all.

Part IV
The Transcendent

What Are You When You Are No More?

If you're someone who feels uncomfortable when thinking about death, then perhaps a glimpse into your eternal nature might put you at ease.

I want you to take a second and think about what it's like to be alive. Right now, you exist, and someday you won't. But what's left of you when you die?

You're able to experience things—to think and to feel. Isn't that cool? The whole universe in all its randomness and complexity conspired to produce you and give you life… and inevitably death. But what'll be left of you once you're gone?

The obvious answer is a corpse. But even that won't exist forever. Your body will decay and eventually your legacy will fade to the erosion of time. Think farther ahead, and think deeper about what it means to be you. Or more specifically, what it means to be *a you*.

You are a thing that isn't just a thing, you're a you. You are a being that is aware of itself. You're also conscious. You're a Self. As far as we know, things with your degree of consciousness are surprisingly rare. A rock doesn't know it exists (or so it seems). Even other animals don't seem to have a full awareness of their life and the strange circumstances underlying their existence. You are a thing that realizes it's a thing. And you also realized that someday you will no longer be a thing.

So what's left of you when you're gone? You'll be gone, but the universe will still be around. Matter will still exist, and the cosmos will keep on doing its thing. The laws of physics and fundamental axioms of logical possibility will continue to exist.

"So what?" you might ask. You're still dead and it doesn't seem like there's anything left of you. At least, nothing left of your physical existence and personal sense of self. But what underlies your sense of self? You are created from reality, which means there are physical laws and processes of nature that work to produce the thing that you are. And once you're gone, these physical laws and processes of nature will still exist.

Where are you, exactly? Are you your brain? Your heart? Your hands and your feet? Are you that which moves your body? Or are you that which is moved? And what's different about your movement than the movement of the cosmos and forces of physics?

In the words of Alan Watts, "If I am my foot, I am the sun. Only we've got this little partial view. We've got the idea that 'No, I'm something *in* this body.'"[137]

If what you are can be reduced to the processes of the cosmos and mechanisms of reality, then it seems that the deepest sense of what you are will continue to exist beyond your bodily death. Although your body is temporary, the structure and the physics of your consciousness are eternal. Your life will end, but that which gives you life will survive after your death. The thing that makes you a "you" will exist after your death, and has existed before your birth.

When considering the eternity that is "you," or more accurately, that which underlies "youness," there's another thought by Alan Watts that I find illuminating. He says, "Imagine what it will be like to go to sleep and never wake up… You will find out, among other things, that it will pose a next question to you: what was it like to wake up after having never gone to sleep?"[138]

That which makes you, you, is built into the fabric of reality. Although you will die, It will remain. The laws of physics, logic, and Possibility, along with the operations of the cosmos and consciousness, are eternal—predating your birth and continuing after your death. What makes you conscious, predates you. What makes you conscious, is you. And what makes you conscious will persist after your death. This is what's left of you after you're gone, and perhaps in some deeper sense, this is what you always were; only you've forgotten your true nature.

Searching For the Strawman: What God Is Not

You've heard it said, "I don't believe in God. It's absurd and far-fetched."

Of course, our idea of God is comically simple. It's a non-physical abstraction that has to be embodied in a character of our story. We have to somehow represent it within our perception of the world.

Whatever God is, it holds together the entire universe and all of reality. Do you really think that the thing that created and regulates the physical universe would just exist as a physical thing in the world? This is as absurd as a magical man in the sky.

When you think of God, if your idea is something similar to the Easter Bunny, Fairies, and the Boogeyman, then perhaps your view of God isn't as rich and comprehensive as the ultimate and eternal power of the universe really is.

It also seems like people want to turn any idea of God into something so laughably simple that of course a serious and meaningful discussion can't be had. So let's stop searching for the strawman and actually entertain the foundational ideas at play.

The Om

What if we merge **Psychology**—the study of the psyche (Greek word for "soul"),[139]

With

Cosmology—the study of the cosmos (Greek word "kosmos" meaning "order of the world").[140]

Merging these two fields of study into one unified approach would make sense if we assumed that consciousness, *and* that which it perceives, are the same thing. What would happen if we investigated *this* as the root of both mind and matter? Would we stumble upon the centre of reality itself?

What is the name of this?

What is it?

What is, the "It"?

The materialists say all there is, is the "it."

The "It" is just "it."

The ancient Hebrews say, the "It" is Being.

The "It" is the "I am." God in the Old Testament is called, "Yahweh," ancient Hebrew for YHWH, which means "I am." This is what God names himself when talking to Moses through the burning bush.[141] In response to Moses asking what he should call him, Yahweh said, "I Am Who I Am." When we utter these words, we are the divine consciousness embodied in humanity.

The Hindus say "It" is composed of two separate things, existing as both the "It" and the "I Am." The Brahman (Sanskrit for 'Ultimate Reality') and the Atman (Sanskrit for 'Self Within').[142] These concepts are two sides of the same coin and are commonly interpreted as matter and mind.

The "It" and the "I am."

Is there anything between the "It" and the "I Am"?

What is this Thing between the subject and the object?

What are the subjective and the objective? Within what vessel is the subjective perceiving the objective?

What is this investigation?

God and gods: The Mutual Truth of Polytheism and Monotheism

A wise person once told me that all religions were like arrows pointing at something beyond them. Focussing on the arrow misses what the arrow is aiming at. Religion can be understood as the specific arrow, and it can also be thought of as what the arrow is pointing at.

A monotheistic God can exist in a polytheistic cosmos. And polytheistic gods don't undermine the reality of The One God. The One can be expressed as many, and The Many are all rooted in The One.

There is The All, which is the totality of everything. And this All is all there is. And there's just one of them. And this one is a One. It just *is* and we have to accept that as Being. Let's call this being, "The One." The One is often conceptualized by monotheists as God. They believe that there is only one God, and He is the creator, architect, and upholder of all reality.

Monotheists are often contrasted with polytheists who believe in multiple gods. Although it may seem intuitive that monotheism and polytheism are incompatible and contradict one another, this is not the case. Monotheism and polytheism can exist together. The truth of monotheism and polytheism are compatible and anchored to the same Transcendent reality. The One can exist in a polytheistic cosmos. Or more accurately stated, polytheistic representations of God as gods don't undermine the existence of The One.

Polytheists are demonstrating that forces of the cosmos exist and represent them symbolically as gods. These gods exist as symbolic representations of cosmic forces and patterns of reality. These forces are of the cosmos. These forces are the operation of the universe. They are an eternal feature of reality that transcends the material world.

Monotheists often misunderstand the belief in polytheistic gods or deities as undermining the belief in The One God. But this is not the case. The gods of polytheism are all manifestations of the same God of monotheism. Polytheism is articulating the Transcendent as multiple rather than singular.

Consider the monotheistic religion of Christianity. Christians suggest that the life of Jesus seems to illuminate the Transcendent. Christians argue that Jesus *is* the Transcendent. Which he is, but he's also the symbolic representation of the Transcendent, so much so that human civilization was rapidly drawn to this message in an archetypical fashion. And Christians have valuable insight when they demonstrate that Jesus is the same thing as The One.

The One is represented through Jesus. And for this to make sense, Jesus is the human embodiment of The One, or The All. Whereas some non-Christians say the All, Christians say The All since the Transcendent is embodied in the specific individual of Jesus Christ.

And this is why some followers of polytheistic religions such as Hinduism easily accepted Christianity when it spread to the East because Eastern thought initially understood Jesus as an embodiment of the Divine. Some Hindus had no issue believing in Jesus as a god since symbolic representations of the Divine through multiple gods are a common feature of Hinduism. Hinduism has many gods, all of which are an embodiment of the Transcendent. But this conception of the Transcendent as gods—forces of the ultimate reality—does not conflict with the notion of a monotheistic God. They are not mutually exclusive.

Polytheism is compatible with Monotheism. Polytheistic gods are symbolic representations of the Divinity of The One God. The One manifests itself in many forms, yet The Many stems from the same Transcendent core. They are both studying the same Transcendent metaphysical reality.

Our world is home to many religions, all believing in a supreme being or beings. Although religions may differ, they all stem the same Transcendent core. All religions are arrows pointing at something beyond themselves. It's not as important which arrow you chose, so long as you focus on what the arrow is aiming at.

Global Theology: Three Types of God

When we think of "God", what do we mean by this?

Well, right off the bat this word means two kinds of gods depending on how you use it.

When "god" is written without a capital, it just refers to any ol' god of the thousands out there. But when "God" is written with a capital, it is a name for a specific god who's assumed to exist as a proper noun.

The Christians will capitalize "God" since there is only one god. But the word "god" is actually of Dutch and Germanic origins, not the Hebrew origins of the Christian god. The ancient Dutch, Germanic, and Mediterranean peoples understood the word "god" to refer to a spirit of the world that was called upon or invoked. Think of the embodied gods of these cultures as representing forces of the world as a spirit. These are the pantheons of the Greeks, Norse, and Hindu peoples.[143]

This is different from the ancient Hebrew understanding of the *only* god and the ultimate nature of reality as YHWH (pronounced "Yahweh"), which means "I am."[144] From Yahweh, also known as the God of Abraham, the religions of Christianity and Islam split off from Judaism, but still trace their lineage and scripture to Abraham and his god. This is why Judaism, Christianity, and Islam are often referred to as "The Abrahamic Religions" since they believe in the same god of Abraham, who they all refer to as "God."

These ideas of God are different from the ancient Eastern conception of the ultimate reality as the Om, which is the combined nature of the Atman (Self Within) and the Brahman (The Universe). This is comparable to another Eastern idea of the Tao, more commonly known as the "Yin/Yang" symbol, which means "the path, way, the flow of the universe, order of the cosmos" and is often translated as "that which can't be put to words" and "eternally nameless."

The Abrahamic religions think that God is One. The pantheists think God is several and represented as the gods who are the spirits of the world and archetypes of consciousness. The ancient Indians thought God was Brahman, and that the true nature of reality is represented by the Om and the Tao.

Notice how there are three types of gods the ancients believed in. Could it be the case that they are all slightly different perspectives of the same Divine reality?

There's God as the One, the "I am," and the ultimate nature of reality. The ultimate ordering principle. That from which order is created from chaos. The rules, the stern, and the patriarchal. The Abrahamic God. Allah. Yahweh. God the Father.

There's God as the spirits of the world, the forces of nature, the embodied spirits, the archetypes of consciousness, and among these archetypes is that type of being which is the most godly and divine, the most godlike god of the pantheists. Zeus. Deus (Latin for "God"). Jesus as the living embodiment of what the ultimate reality would look like through a person. God the Son.

And then there's God as the nature of reality, both the forces of the universe and the patterns of consciousness. The Atman and the Brahman. That which is not only embodied but is transcendent and pervades all. Cosmic order. The Force. The flow of the Universe. The Om. The Tao. The underlying Divinity in all of reality. God the Holy Spirit.

Is it just a coincidence that the Christian Holy Trinity maps onto the three different conceptions of the Divine? Could it be that an early sect of Christianity wanted to integrate the various religions across the known world into an *updated* theology, incorporating the beliefs of the Sacred and Divine from most cultures of their time? Christianity emerged from a multitude of religions in some of the most multicultural regions of the ancient world. Would we be naïve to think Christianity didn't incorporate that which came before it into a synthesis of Divine understanding?

The Transcendent

It seems that the world's major religions' understanding of God and the Divine matches the description of what's experienced during the mystical experience that often accompanies psychedelic use. Those who undergo a mystical experience (also called a religious or transcendent experience) find it difficult to put into words, but often report a feeling of loving bliss and ultimate oneness with all things, a sense of their consciousness extending beyond their physical body, and pure awareness of the ultimate reality.[145]

The insights people gain from an encounter with a mystical experience are overwhelmingly positive, often helping one re-conceptualize their relationships, traumas, and sense of purpose. The introspective awareness of the mystical experience is what makes it so effective in the rapidly evolving field of psychedelic-assisted therapy. When coupled with professional psychotherapy in a safe and controlled setting, encountering a mystical experience has been demonstrated to be an effective treatment for addiction, depression, anxiety, and PTSD.[146]

Given the subjective description of the mystical experience along with its mental and emotional benefits, is it unreasonable to speculate that the mystical experience induced by psychedelics could be an encounter with God?

Part V
Prosperity

The Ultimate Aim

I wanted to be a comedian, so I could bring people joy and make them laugh.

I wanted to be a priest, so I could help bring people to God's love.

I wanted to be a lawyer, so I could serve justice.

I wanted to be a police officer, so I could help my community by maintaining law and order.

I wanted to be a UN peacekeeper, so I could defend the innocent and stand for peace.

I wanted to be an electrician, so I could do honest work and provide energy for our society.

I wanted to be a high school teacher, so I could educate and mentor the next generation.

I wanted to be a politician, so I could create smart policy, make good decisions, and be a leader for the people.

I wanted to be an entrepreneur, so I could bring innovation and prosperity to my society.

I wanted to be a community leader, so I could bring people together.

I wanted to be a motivational speaker, so I could help people become their best.

I wanted to be a researcher, so I could advance our knowledge and bring us closer to the truth.

I wanted to be a professor, so I could inspire students through the experience of their field.

I wanted to be a mystic, so I could bring people in contact with the Divine.

I wanted to be a therapist, so I could help people find themselves and become whole.

I wanted to be a financial planner, so I could help people become wealthy and financially independent.

I don't know what I want to be, but I know I want to be a good one. And no matter what I do, so long as I aim at The Good, then I know it'll be the right choice.

What are you Building?

To Those Who Are Just Showing Up and Putting in Time
The Fruits of Flourishing

>Punch in. Do nothing. Punch out.
>Show up. Do nothing. Go home.

>Rinse. Repeat.

Just show up, punch in, not care, go home. There's too much of this. Too much neglect and apathy. Too much avoidance and laziness. To those of you who just put in time, I say this:

I call you leeches. You lazy dogs who would fake being sick so you could be supported by the pack. If only you knew you could lead the pack.

I feel pity for you. I'm sad for you that you've never been able to have a fulfilling day at work. It pains me to see you ache to go home and suffer throughout your day. Perhaps you don't want to work, perhaps you don't know how, perhaps you don't see a reason to. I feel bad for you. All of you. You lazy miserable dogs. You don't see it, do you? If only you knew you could be wolves.

Look around, you see it too. Too many people not putting in the work. Perhaps you're one of them. This is not a good way to live. There's nothing life-like about it—just waiting and decaying. Those who just put in time are in a constant struggle against the clock.

Don't just show up. Don't just waste time and watch the clock for when you can go home. Get things done! Add value. Make something great. You can do this wherever you are, from retail, school, factory work, etc. Prosperity will never be created from a half-ass attitude. You must want to create greatness for greatness to manifest. Imagine how good things could be if we stop putting in time and just got to work.

Whatever you're doing, see through it. Look beyond what you're doing to find out *why*. Then aim at that goal. People often hate their job but they don't do anything throughout the day. If people see the purpose in what they're doing and make it their mission to do a good job, then they won't be miserable throughout the day. You just have to want the goal you're aiming at. Derive satisfaction from working by adding value.

People waste so much time trying to look busy. They're making unnecessary calls, sending useless emails, and walking around pretending to work. Why waste time pretending to work when you can actually work? It's funny because when you actually work, the day goes by quicker. When you actually work and lose yourself in what you're doing, before you know it, it's time to go home. When you have things to do and tasks to achieve, you're no longer staring down the clock waiting to punch out. When you cultivate an attitude of wanting to do good work wherever you go, time moves differently. Your day becomes a race against the clock, a challenge of how much value you can add before you go home.

When you slack off, you add negativity to the world. You actively make the world worse with your attitude and actions. Just putting in time is to avoid doing that which needs to be done. The responsibilities you avoid ultimately fall onto someone else. Your clients' and customers' lives are made worse when you don't care about their experience. Your coworkers' lives are made worse when you don't care about their experience.

Human flourishing comes to those who lay the foundation for its thriving. By slacking off and not giving a job your heart, you spit in the face of what your organization could become. You spit in the face of the prosperity you could build.

When you care about prosperity, your day is enriched. You positively affect your clients and customers. You make the lives of your co-workers better. Everybody wins. You spread uplifting and good ripples out into the world. Your workday isn't just a way to get money, it's an opportunity to add value to the world. You earn money in exchange for value produced. You'll never earn more money if you don't add more value.

"The harvest is plentiful but the workers are few (Matt 9:37)." The potential for prosperity is all around us, but people don't see it. All that is needed is to aim at doing good to reap the fruits of flourishing.

"The kingdom of heaven is spread upon the earth, but men do not see it (Thomas 113)."[147] If only we realized in ourselves and all around us the ability to create prosperity, then we would have Heaven on Earth.

We choose what lives and dies. We are evolution. We are life and death.

Every day, every action, every choice, we decide what's important for us to put out into the world. We choose what lives on.

What values do you choose to pass on? What are you building?

To those of you who just show up, to those of you who just put in time, I ask you, what do you choose to carry on? What values and attitudes do you choose to put into the world?

I choose to work hard.

I choose attitudes that foster goodness and success. I choose the path to community wellbeing and human flourishing.

I choose the principles of prosperity.

What is Your Life a Monument to?

If your life is a thing that you're building, what would it be?

What is it? What will it be when it's done?

Is your life a brothel and buffet for pleasure?

Would your life be a machine of obedience?

If your life is something to be built, would it be a house of knowledge for the treaties of truth? Would it be the halls of power?

Is your life a city on a hill—a light of the world that cannot be hidden?

Is it something soft, warm, and comforting?

Is it something rigid, hard, and enduring?

Is what you're building a community where peace, harmony, and freedom exist for all?

Would your life be that of a strong tyrannical state or dictator?

Would your life be a rebellion against oppression, fighting for a world of liberty and opportunity for all?

Or, would your life be something internal? Is it a journey to embark on alone?

Perhaps your life is a journey, but is it a journey to be made with others?

With your life, are you building an ark to withstand the waters of the coming flood?

Is your life something that can illuminate the darkness?

Is it a tower to God?

Is your life something that can turn things into gold?

Most importantly, is whatever you're building, something worth building?

Mind and Placebo

Are we a material brain or an immaterial mind? Some say that the mind is controlled by the brain—that all we are is a complex intricacy of particles and electrical impulses.

Sure, the brain has influence over the mind. Our moods can be influenced by ingesting a substance or receiving a pharmaceutical drug. It's possible to take into our body something that will alter our physical make-up which affects our mental experience.

But what's interesting is how our mental experience can affect our physical brain. The placebo effect occurs in instances where we receive a dummy/empty substance while thinking that it will have a certain effect, and then this effect occurs. It seems the expectation of a result, or the thoughts of the mind, will cause a physiological response in the human brain. Even though the placebo effect is used in clinical studies to compare the effectiveness of a pharmaceutical intervention, modern science is unable to explain why it occurs.[148]

Why can the immaterial mind influence the material brain? How is it that our thoughts can change our body? Is it even possible to be fully constrained by the matter of our brain if our mind can exert influence over our physiological composition?

Is the mind truly confined by the brain? It doesn't seem so. It seems the mind is able to influence the brain rather than the brain constraining the mind.

Mental transfiguration is the art of changing mental states of the mind. If the mind is unconstrained by the brain, then what holds the mind back from changing how it feels? Those who have mastered the art of mental transfiguration say nothing truly holds back the mind. Not biology, not the brain, nothing except for the mind itself.

The state you seek already exists. Written into the cosmos is every emotion and state of mind. They are there for you to access and attain through a transformative experience. You need only think, and you will become. Are you that which is moved, or are you that which does the moving? The life of a domino in a causal chain is not the life of the mind. You are not your mood; you are your mind. The mind is above the laws of cause and effect. The mind is the cause of causation.

In the words of Tony Robbins, "Where focus goes, energy flows."[149] The most valuable wisdom is knowing how to direct our mind. Our mind is powerful. Our mind doesn't just determine the quality of our thoughts, but the physical contents of our brain. What we think, we become. What are you going to think about? What are you going to become?

But you are imperfect. You will often forget your true nature and return to being a pawn in the cosmic game. You will be moved by forces seemingly outside of yourself and forget that it is you who does the moving.

Alchemy and the Elixir of Life

Extract The Gold and Make It Good
The prosperity principle is to become that which makes life good.

Live your life in such a way that you bring goodness and prosperity to all that you touch. Be like a torch in a cave that illuminates all that surrounds it wherever it moves. Become a light in the darkness, be the light unto the world. Make things better. And when they threaten to get worse, resist the growing darkness. Maintain the light and become an agent of the good. The meaning of life is to make things good, while also accepting that which is beyond your control.

The meaning of life is an alchemical myth; to transform yourself into something capable of turning the world into gold while going with life's flow and acknowledging the darkness in the light. Despite life's suffering and tragedy essential to existence, the meaning of life is to work for the good anyway. To build, create, and maintain goodness is our ultimate calling. We are those who build prosperity out of whatever situation we encounter. Make more goodness in the world and lessen the badness. The meaning of life is to be an agent of goodness.

In every moment, act as if someone has handed you a torch in the darkness and ask yourself, where am I going with this? Where will I spread this light? Who will I bring it to and where will this potential for goodness be actualized? And then go do it as both your most important ethical responsibility and your deepest desire.

Parable of the Sower

Again Jesus began to teach by the lake. The crowd that gathered around him was so large that he got into a boat and sat in it out on the lake, while all the people were along the shore at the water's edge. He taught them many things by parables, and in his teaching said: "Listen! A farmer went out to sow his seed. As he was scattering the seed, some fell along the path, and the birds came and ate it up. Some fell on rocky places, where it did not have much soil. It sprang up quickly, because the soil was shallow. But when the sun came up, the plants were scorched, and they withered because they had no root. Other seed fell among thorns, which grew up and choked the plants, so that they did not bear grain. Still other seed fell on good soil. It came up, grew and produced a crop, some multiplying thirty, some sixty, some a hundred times." Then Jesus said, "Whoever has ears to hear, let them hear."

(Mark 4:1-9)

The Cure For Anxiety

Therefore I tell you, do not be anxious about your life, what you will eat or what you will drink, nor about your body, what you will put on. Is not life more than food, and the body more than clothing? Look at the birds of the air: they neither sow nor reap nor gather into barns, and yet your heavenly Father feeds them. Are you not of more value than they? And which of you by being anxious can add a single hour to their span of life? And why are you anxious about clothing? Consider the lilies of the field, how they grow: they neither toil nor spin, yet I tell you, even Solomon in all his glory was not arrayed like one of these. But if God so clothes the grass of the field, which today is alive and tomorrow is thrown into the oven, will he not much more clothe you, O you of little faith? Therefore do not be anxious, saying, 'What shall we eat?' or 'What shall we drink?' or 'What shall we wear?' For the Gentiles seek after all these things, and your heavenly Father knows that you need them all. But seek first the kingdom of God and his righteousness, and all these things will be added to you.

Therefore do not be anxious about tomorrow, for tomorrow will be anxious for itself. Sufficient for the day is its own trouble.

(Matthew 6:25-34)

Prosperity and Human Flourishing

Doesn't the tree exist in the seed?

Don't the patterns of the cosmos exist in all things?

So isn't it also true that prosperity exists all around us in the potential and possibility of this world?

Let she who has ears, hear. And let he who has eyes, see.

You are not nothing. You are not pawns to be moved by politicians, corporations, or the whims of nature. You are not lifeless matter in a meaningless void.

Truly I tell you, We are Life itself.

We are the forces of nature. We are evolution. We chose what lives and dies. Every day, every action, and every choice, we decide what's important for us to put out into the world.

The Altar of Relaxation

Our couches have become an altar to the gods of relaxation while we sacrifice our body and soul. Somewhere along the line, our culture began to make relaxation the goal of our days.

Putting your feet up and *resting* is celebrated as the pinnacle of what one should be doing. Why work? That's hard. Moving requires work, and there's an idea out there that *work* should be avoided. Shortcuts, doing nothing, and relaxing have become the aim of human fulfillment.

No wonder our culture is so depressed. And no wonder our culture is so unhealthy. Depression and mental health issues are our biggest hindrances while living,[150] and sedentary conditions such as heart disease are the most common path to our graves.[151] Something in our lifestyle is killing both our body and soul. I suspect our obsession with comfort and relaxation is at least partially to blame.

There's an old saying, "If you rest, you rust."[152] This is true mentally and physically. Somewhere along the way, we decided that to come home and *relax* is how we should lead our lives and derive our fulfillment.

The body is powered by *will*, not rest. The mind is refreshed by creation, connection, and engagement, not pampered relaxation.

"But we're tired", they say. "We must rest." They have no energy to do anything, and they have no energy *because* they don't do anything. Your body has energy—lots of it. With proper sleep, healthy food, and purpose, you'll have energy to spare. It's a cruel irony of our modern age that our lazy and restful lifestyle makes us more drained and exhausted.

The mind and body are linked, and both the mind and body need a purpose. We need something to do. We need something to get us up and working. Not work in a slavish or brutal sense, but in a liberating expression of one's soul. Whether it be your job, exercise, hobby, or craft, working is anything that gets you doing something and fully engaging with the world. This lifestyle of welcoming work is the antithesis of resting, but is the cure for our exhaustion. We're not tired because we work, we're tired because we're forgotten *why* we work. We work because it is what humanity is meant for. Work is what humanity has evolved for. Work is where we find our purpose. There's no greater fulfillment than to engage with the world, with both our mind and body towards a higher purpose.

Only after this kind of work can we justify relaxation. And only after this kind of work will our minds be at ease. Now chose a purpose, get off the couch, and get to work, or face the inevitable rusting of relaxation.

The Hero's Journey

There's a story that humans have told one another for as long as we have written and oral records. There's one story that keeps popping up in every civilization across all of history. This one story has outlived the rise and fall of empires. This story has survived an ice age and had been with our ancestors for as far back as we can trace our ancient origins. This story emerges independent of the time and location. Wherever there are humans, this story is found. For over twenty thousand years this story has accompanied our species. In some sense, this story is an extension of our human nature and the most fundamental representation of the human experience. This story is the unifying core of all mythology. This is the story that unites the human race. This is *The Hero's Journey*.

What's interesting about *The Hero's Journey* and stories that share its pattern is that it seems to come from our unconscious mind. Not only do we resonate with and recognize the classic hero tale, but we find it *everywhere*. Of course, there are distinct differences in the unique characteristics of a story, similar to how different clothes are worn by the same person, but what's underneath the outer differences remains the same. It's not a coincidence that thousands of civilizations separated by thousands of years and thousands of miles produced the same story.

Modern stories like Harry Potter, Star Wars, and The Lord of The Rings, all echo this timeless tale that mirrors stories from ancient Egyptian mythology, Mesopotamian creation myths, and European epics. These same stories appear across the Americas, Africa, and throughout Asia. While the differences between these stories are minor, the similarities are essentially human.

The tides of history will bring change and the patterns of the social world will unfold. A shadow will fall over the kingdom, but a new dawn will come.

Against the forces of darkness, the hero can bring the light. It seems that this is the story told by the human mind wherever and whenever it exists.

After recognizing similarities across the mythologies from all human cultures, an American professor of mythology, Dr. Joseph Campbell, coined the term "*The Monomyth*" and "*The Hero's Journey*" to describe the essential features of the human species' most common story. His central finding was that tales of heroism appear across all cultures and time periods, depicting the hero and their struggle against adversity as fundamental to human consciousness.[153]

Perhaps this story is about how the human mind perceives and experiences reality. Following this thought, if our experience of the world is limited to our mind, then this story *is* reality.

And both the story and reality seem to say this:

The spirit of heroism lives on throughout the ages in the minds and hearts of human beings. Heroism itself is eternal and brings luminous life out from the darkness of the underworld. The stories of heroism across all civilizations say the same thing—problems and suffering are eternal, but human beings can triumph over whatever adversity they face.

We are the light in the darkness.

Necessity

I've seen the light. I've seen the darkness. I've soared through the heights of Heaven and descended downwards into the fires of Hell. I've climbed mountains and been swallowed by the abyss. And I realized that within darkness there is light.

Through the light, there is darkness. The light will not always be there. But it will return. Even the nights that are darkest eventually turn into day.

Necessity is the origin of all growth. It is only when we succumb to fire that we can grow wings. In the words of Carl Jung, "No tree, it is said, can grow to heaven unless its roots reach down to hell."[154] In the darkness, there is light, a light that the human being can shine unto the world.

The Hero's Vow

I swear myself to this oath to Goodness, this service to Virtue, and to this testament to heroism for as long as I play a character on this stage.

...

I commit myself to the standards of honesty, integrity, and courage. To defend values that affirm the life and the vitality of human civilization.

To further justice, peace, and prosperity.

To swear myself to human flourishing as the ultimate ideal.

To live in harmony with the forces of good. And to defend against the forces of evil. To see the humanity in my opponents and to recognize the part of myself in all life. To recognize that perceived evil often manifests as ignorance, incompetence, and apathy, and to encourage their opposites.

To regard my family as my immediate and closest community. To view this network as the core of my tribe and country. To view the health of this network as essential to the prosperity of the whole.

To regard communities of individuals and families as the literal web that unites all life. To see communities as the vessels we build to survive the coming floods.

To keep myself in prime physical health, to always be ready for war and physical confrontation. To always be capable of fighting for defence and the protection of the weak. To be capable of handling any tragedy, emergency, or natural disaster. To stave off war and famine whenever they arrive on my doorstep.

To prioritize my financial and economic power. To make sure I always have the means of being able to offer help if needed. To make sure I have the economic means of being a positive influence in my communities and our larger society. To prioritize my financial situation so I can be generous and wise with my resources; so I can plant gardens for future generations to enjoy;

so I can use my wealth to plant trees whose shade I'll never get to sit under. To acknowledge my ethical obligation to do this and to strive for its fulfillment. To become an economic force for good in this world.

To take care of my mental and cognitive health. To retain sharpness of mind and clarity, and use it in the pursuit of truth over deception or trickery. To regard truth as the ultimate basis for reality and the giver of all things that grow stable and strong. To view the truth as illuminating and the bearer of good fruit, and something that awakens and builds good things.

To recognize the good in what another is saying and to work in good faith where possible.

To align myself with harmony over disease. To further health over illness. And to serve vitality over decay.

To challenge error where possible and push back against matters of conscience and moral obligation.

To prevent the accumulation of too much power over society and maintain organizations against corruption, directing institutions towards goodness and wellbeing.

To oppose tyranny, oppression, and unnecessary coercion against the luminous thriving of human freedom. To resist barriers of arbitrary or unnecessary limitation on one's opportunity to lead a life of excellence and their most meaningful fulfillment.

To further heroism over cowardliness, adventure over boredom, prosperity over corruption, and growth over sterility.

To regard the experience of goodness as paramount, but to acknowledge the bad as necessary for goodness and growth. To prioritize the wellbeing of the community as my fundamental ethical obligation.

To acknowledge my flaws with humility and loving judgement. To always strive to exist in harmony with others and be forgiving and loving in my dealings wherever possible. But to not unduly put the wellbeing of others above my own dignity and importance.

To take responsibility for bettering my flaws as my moral obligation to the wellbeing of my social networks and communities.

...

To dare to live by this oath at all times, even in times when it becomes difficult or uncomfortable, especially when it becomes difficult or uncomfortable. To dare to live this path over a life of apathy, convenience, or bitterness of spirit.

To dedicate myself to excellence. To serve Goodness in a way that is productive to reap the largest harvest and the Best fruit.

To be a light in the darkness, a port in the distance, and to embody a shining city of a hill, spreading light unto the world.

Endnotes

[1] Friedrich Nietzsche, translated by Adrian Del Caro. *Thus Spoke Zarathustra*. "On Priests." Cambridge University Press, New York, 2006. p. 71.

[2] Unknown origins of this quote. It has been attributed to Mark Twain, Agatha Christie, and Sally Berger. I credit Mark Twain in the text since this was how the quote was credited when I first came across the phrase. Either way, the sentiment is very wise and regardless of who first said it, it was not me.

[3] "recreation (n.)." *Online Etymology Dictionary*. https://www.etymonline.com/word/recreation.

[4] Ibid.

[5] HBO. *Game of Thrones*. Season two. Episode one. "The North Remembers." First aired April 1st, 2012.

[6] Sun Tzu, and Samuel B. Griffith. *The Art of War*. Shelter Harbor Press, 2016. p. 56.

[7] Aristotle. *The Politics*. 1253a.

[8] HBO. *Game of Thrones*. Season two. Episode one. "The North Remembers." First aired April 1st, 2012.

[9] Carl Jung. *Aion: Researches into the Phenomenology of the Self*. Chapter five. Princeton University Press, 1970, second edition. p. 43.

[10] Friedrich Nietzsche, translated by Adrian Del Caro. *Thus Spoke Zarathustra*. Cambridge University Press, New York, 2006. p. 9.

[11] Walt Whitman. *Leaves of Grass*. "O Me! O Life!" 1892.

[12] Other sources from Hesiod, Apollodorus, and other authors disagree with this claim, instead suggesting that humans were only created be Prometheus or that Prometheus was the benefactor of humanity rather than its creator. It's commonly referenced in contemporary accounts that the creation of humanity was a joint effort between Prometheus and Athena. Such an account can be found at greekmythology.com, and https://www.greekmythology.com/Titans/Prometheus/prometheus.html.

[13] "Prometheus." *Encyclopedia Britannica*. https://www.britannica.com/topic/Prometheus-Greek-god.

[14] "Athena." *Encyclopedia Britannica*. https://www.britannica.com/topic/Athena-Greek-mythology. Additional information found at, https://www.desy.de/gna/interpedia/greek_myth/olympian.html#Athena.

[15] Hattie WH. The caduceus. Can Med Assoc J. 1928;18:79–80. https://www.ncbi.nlm.nih.gov/pmc/articles/PMC1709497/pdf/canmedaj00472-0135.pdf.

[16] "Mercury (Deity)." *World History Encyclopedia*. https://www.worldhistory.org/Mercury_(Deity)/.

[17] One such example of the myth can be found in a summary here, https://classicalwisdom.com/culture/the-caduceus-magical-staff-of-hermes/.

[18] Hattie WH. The caduceus. Can Med Assoc J. 1928;18:79–80. https://www.ncbi.nlm.nih.gov/pmc/articles/PMC1709497/pdf/canmedaj00472-0135.pdf.

[19] United States Environmental Protection Agency. Artisanal and Small-Scale Gold Mining Without Mercury. https://www.epa.gov/international-cooperation/artisanal-and-small-scale-gold-mining-without-mercury#:~:text=In%20many%20countries%2C%20elemental%20mercury,mercury%20to%20obtain%20the%20gold.

[20] Lao Tzu, translated by Stephen Mitchell. *Tao Te Ching*. Verse 76. Harper Collins Publishers, New York, 1988. p. 76.

[21] Bruce Lee. *Longstreet*. 1971.

[22] "lucifer." *Oxford Learner's Dictionary*. https://www.oxfordlearnersdictionaries.com/definition/english/lucifer.

[23] Holy Bible. Revelation. 12:7-9.

[24] Bishop Robert Barron and Lex Fridman. "Bishop Robert Barron: Christianity and the Catholic Church | Lex Fridman Podcast #304." Timestamp 22:40. July 20th, 2022. https://www.youtube.com/watch?v=WgytXF0SPh0.

[25] "idea (n.)." *Online Etymology Dictionary*. https://www.etymonline.com/word/idea.

[26] Mark Cartwright. "Shiva." *World History Encyclopedia*. May 10th, 2018. https://www.worldhistory.org/shiva/.

[27] Same Littlefair. "Was Yoda based on this Buddhist master?" Lions Roar. May 5th, 2015. https://www.lionsroar.com/was-yoda-based-on-this-buddhist-master/.

[28] George Lucas. *Star Wars: A New Hope*. Lucasfilm Ltd. Released May 25th, 1977.

[29] Livia Kohn. *The Taoist Experience: An Anthology*. Published by State University of New York Press, Albany, 1983. p 11.

And, Lao Tzu, translated by Stephen Mitchell. *Tao Te Ching*. Verse 2. Harper Collins Publishers, New York, 1988. p. 1.

[30] George Lucas. *Star Wars: Episode I – The Phantom Menace*. Lucasfilm Ltd. Released May 19th, 1999.

[31] Paul Duncan. "The Star Wars Archives: 1999-2005." Taschen, Germany, 2020.

[32] Stanford Encyclopedia of Philosophy. "Buddha." Feb 14th, 2019. https://plato.stanford.edu/entries/buddha/.

[33] Viktor Frankl. *Man's Search For Meaning*. Preface by Gordon Allport. Beacon Press, 1992. p. 9.

[34] Charlie Chaplin. *The Great Dictator*. 1940. Final Speech.

[35] Lao Tzu, translated by Stephen Mitchell. *Tao Te Ching*. Verse 2. Harper Collins Publishers, New York, 1988. p. 2.

[36] The origin of this quote is worded slightly different than it was employed. It seems that the quote changed as it spread throughout the culture over time, or that when Jospeh Campbell spoke, which he often did during interviews, lectures, and speeches, he may have altered the quote. Either way, the sentiment remains the same and is attributed to Joseph Cambell which he credits to countless mythologies. Jospeh Campbell. Reflections on the Art of Living: A Joseph Campbell Companion, Selected and edited by Diane K. Osbon. HarperCollins, New York, 1991. p. 8 and 24.

[37] Carl Jung. *Mysterium Coniunctionis: An Inquiry into the Separation and Synthesis of Psychic Opposites in Alchemy*. Epilogue. Princeton University Press, 1977. p. 653.

[38] Jordan Peterson. *Maps of Meaning*. Routledge, 1999. p. 405.

[39] Christopher Perry. "The Jungian Shadow." Society of Analytical Psychology. Aug 12th, 2015. https://www.thesap.org.uk/articles-on-jungian-psychology-2/about-analysis-and-therapy/the-shadow/.

[40] Carl Jung. *Psychology and Alchemy*. Chapter three. Princeton University Press, 1980. para. 208.

[41] Carl Jung. *Alchemical Studies*. Chapter five. Princeton University Press, 1970. p. 265-266.

[42] Friedrich Nietzsche, translated by Richard Polt. *Twilight of the Idols*. Epigrams and Arrows, number twelve. Hackett Publishing Company Inc, Indiana, 1997. p. 6.

[43] "phoenix." *Encyclopedia Britannica*. https://www.britannica.com/topic/phoenix-mythological-bird.

[44] "ideology." *Oxford Learner's Dictionary*. https://www.oxfordlearnersdictionaries.com/definition/english/ideology.

[45] "In situations of high stress, fear or distrust, the hormone and neurotransmitter cortisol floods the brain. Executive functions that help us with advanced thought processes like strategy, trust building, and compassion shut down. And the amygdala, our instinctive brain, takes over. The body makes a chemical choice about how best to protect itself — in this case from the shame and loss of power associated with being wrong — and as a result is unable to regulate its emotions or handle the gaps between expectations and reality. So we default to one of four responses: fight (keep arguing the point), flight (revert to, and hide behind, group consensus), freeze (disengage from the argument by shutting up) or appease (make nice with your adversary by simply agreeing with him)." Excerpt from, Judith E. Glaser. "Your Brain is Hooked on Being Right." *Harvard Business Review*. Feb 28th, 2013. https://hbr.org/2013/02/break-your-addiction-to-being.

[46] Marcus Tullius Cicero. *On the Republic*. "Book Three." 22:33. http://www.attalus.org/cicero/republic3.html.

[47] Jordan Peterson. *The Psychological Significance of the Biblical Stories: Genesis*. "Lecture: Biblical Series III: God and the Hierarchy of Authority." Timestamp 1:37:12-1:38:24. *YouTube*. Jun 6th, 2017. https://www.youtube.com/watch?v=R_GPAl_q2QQ&list=PL22J3VaeABQD_IZs7y60I3lUrrFTzkpat&index=3.

[48] https://oracleofbacon.org/.

⁴⁹ John Donne. *Devotions upon Emergent* Occasions. "XVII. MEDITATION." no. 17. The University of Michigan Press. 1959. p. 108–109. Originally published in 1624.

⁵⁰ For more information, https://aynrand.org/ideas/overview/. Also see her most famous works, *Atlas Shrugged* and *The Fountainhead*.

⁵¹ Jean-Paul Sartre. *Existentialism is a Humanism*. Lecture given in 1946. https://www.marxists.org/reference/archive/sartre/works/exist/sartre.htm. Also found in, Walter Kaufman. *Existentialism from Dostoyevsky to Sartre*. Meridian Publishing Company, 1989.

⁵² J. R. R. Tolkien. *The Lord of the Rings*. Harper Collins Publishers, London, 2004. *The Fellowship of the Ring*. "The Shadow of the Past." p. 51.

⁵³ Quote of unknown origins.

⁵⁴ Peter Jackson. *The Hobbit: An Unexpected Journey*. Film. Released Dec 3ʳᵈ, 2012. Story by J. R. R. Tolkien.

⁵⁵ J. R. R. Tolkien. Edited by Christopher Tolkien. *The Silmarillion*. "AINULINDALË." HarperCollins, London, 1977.

⁵⁶ R. F. Stalley. *Socratic Aporia*. The Classical Review, 53(1), 2003, 48-49. doi:10.1093/cr/53.1.48.

⁵⁷ Johan Norberg. *Progress*. Oneworld Publications, London, 2016.

And, Tristin Hopper. "Hate capitalism? Here's how it keeps lifting millions out of poverty." *The National Post*. Dec 16ᵗʰ, 2021. https://nationalpost.com/news/world/the-capitalist-manifesto-hate-capitalism-too-bad-it-keeps-lifting-millions-out-of-poverty.

⁵⁸ Thomas Piketty. *Capital in the Twenty First Century*. Belknap Press: An Imprint of Harvard University Press, Cambridge MA, 2014.

⁵⁹ Carol R. Ember. *Hunter Gatherers (Foragers)*. "Complex Hunter Gatherers." Jun 1ˢᵗ, 2020. Explaining Human Culture. A database produced by the Human Relations Area Files (HRAF) at Yale University. https://hraf.yale.edu/ehc/summaries/hunter-gatherers.

[60] The World Bank. "Inequality and Violent Crime." *The Journal of Law and Economics*. August 2001. https://web.worldbank.org/archive/website01241/WEB/IMAGES/INEQUALI.PDF.

[61] Ibid.

[62] Susan Stamberg. "How Andrew Carnegie Turned His Fortune Into A Library Legacy." *NPR*. Aug 1st, 2013. https://www.npr.org/2013/08/01/207272849/how-andrew-carnegie-turned-his-fortune-into-a-library-legacy. This source is an example of how the wealthy elite donate their fortune back into their communities. This source isn't exhaustive, though it highlights a case study similar to countless instances of philanthropy and reinvestment on behalf of wealthy elites.

[63] Sarah Bond. "Investing In Infrastructure: Funding Roads In Ancient Rome And Today." *Forbes*. Jun 30th, 2017. https://www.forbes.com/sites/drsarahbond/2017/06/30/investing-in-infrastructure-funding-roads-in-ancient-rome-and-today/?sh=1d04da5b5f83.

[64] René R. Gadacz. *Potlatch*. "Purpose." The Canadian Encyclopedia. October 24th, 2019. https://www.thecanadianencyclopedia.ca/en/article/potlatch#:~:text=Historically%2C%20the%20potlatch%20functioned%20to,individuals%20over%20time%2C%20sometimes%20years.

[65] To my disappointment, this passage I have quoted no longer exists on Sabaton's website. Though to my enjoyment, it seems the band has updated the historical account, providing a more fulsome depiction of historical events. I should've anticipated these history enthusiasts to come out with something more thorough than the previous brief summary. This passage better summarizes the context of the song without having to quote several paragraphs. I'd encourage you the read up on it yourself and even listen to the song, *Hearts of Iron*. Sabaton. "Battle of Berlin Ends." https://www.sabaton.net/historical-facts/battle-of-berlin-ends/.

[66] Both quotes have been attributed to Abraham Lincoln in writings and popular culture since the 1960's, however an original source for either cannot be located. Perhaps these quotes were spoken instead of written and then began to circulate through conversation. Alternatively, Lincoln may never have said either of these quotes, though the ideas that these quotes express seem to reflect the historical consensus of Lincoln's character which could explain why the quotes are attributed to him.

[67] Ibid.

[68] Kevin M. Cherry. "Does Aristotle Believe Greeks Should Rule Barbarians?" *History of Political Thought*. Vol. 35, No. 4 (Winter 2014). p. 632-655. Published by Imprint Academic Ltd. https://www.jstor.org/stable/26226780.

[69] Bethany Minelle. "MLK/FBI: 'They thought his illicit affairs would destroy him… but the press wouldn't touch it'." *Sky News*. Jan 17th, 2021. https://news.sky.com/story/mlk-fbi-they-thought-his-illicit-affairs-would-destroy-him-but-the-press-wouldnt-touch-it-12181421.

[70] "It has been said, 'Anyone who divorces his wife must give her a certificate of divorce.' But I tell you that anyone who divorces his wife, except for sexual immorality, makes her the victim of adultery, and anyone who marries a divorced woman commits adultery." Holy Bible. Matthew 5:31-32 NIV.

[71] Though it should be noted that engaging in racism might have been done for Gandhi's success as a lawyer in South Africa where such racist rhetoric was commonplace. Soutik Biswas. "Was Mahatma Gandhi a racist?." *BBC News*. Sep 17th, 2017. https://www.bbc.com/news/world-asia-india-34265882.

[72] In my opinion, the fact the founding fathers owned slaves is very ironic because their model of government was (literally) revolutionary for its time, focussing on individual freedoms and separation from the tyrannical power structure of the British Empire.
Mark Maloy. "The Founding Fathers View of Slavery." *The Battlefield Trust*. Feb 1st, 2022. https://www.battlefields.org/learn/articles/founding-fathers-views-slavery#:~:text=Many%20of%20the%20major%20Founding,families%2C%20such%20as%20Alexander%20Hamilton.

[73] Solomon F. Bloom. "Karl Marx and the Jews." *Jewish Social Studies*. Vol. 4, No. 1 (Jan 1942), p. 3-16. Indiana University Press. https://www.jstor.org/stable/4615185.

[74] George Orwell. *1984*. Penguin Books, London, 2008.

[75] Plato. *The Republic*. "Book III."

[76] When averaging 10% annual interest, https://www.calculator.net/investment-calculator.html.

[77] Joshua J. Mark. "Athens." *World History Encyclopedia*. July 6th, 2021. https://www.worldhistory.org/Athens/.

[78] Thucydides. *The History of the Peloponnesian War*. Also quoted in Friedrich Nietzsche. *On the Genealogy of Morals*. "First Essay." Section 11.

[79] John A. Shedd. *Salt From My Attic*. The Mosher Press, Portland, Maine, 1928. p. 20.

[80] Robert I. Fitzhenry. *Barnes & Noble Book of Quotations: Revised and Enlarged*. Barnes & Noble Books, Division of Harper & Row, New York, 1987. p. 212.

[81] Lucius Seneca. *On the Shortness of Life*. "Chapter VII." Edited by Stephen Abbott. Abbott ePublishing, 2009. p. 22.

[82] Lucius Seneca. *Letters from a Stoic*. "Letter IV – On the terrors of death." Translated by A. Snow. 20th Century Publishing, 2021. p. 7.

And, Lucius Seneca. *On the Terrors of Death*. "Letter IV." Para 3. translated by Richard Mott Gummere. https://monadnock.net/seneca/4.html.

[83] Franklin D. Roosevelt. *Inaugural Address*. Washington, DC. March 4th, 1933.

[84] Hannah Ritchie, Max Roser and Pablo Rosad. "Crop Yields." Our World in Data. 2022. https://ourworldindata.org/crop-yields.

[85] North American Forest Commission. "State of Forestry in the United States of America." *Food and Agriculture Organization of the United Nations*. 2000. https://www.fao.org/3/x4995e/x4995e.htm.

[86] Trevor Nace. "NASA Says Earth Is Greener Today Than 20 Years Ago Thanks To China, India." *Forbes*. Feb 28th, 2019. https://www.forbes.com/sites/trevornace/2019/02/28/nasa-says-earth-is-greener-today-than-20-years-ago-thanks-to-china-india/?sh=4dcbbf086e13.

[87] Nate Aden. "The Roads to Decoupling: 21 Countries Are Reducing Carbon Emissions While Growing GDP." *World Resources Institute*. April 5th, 2016. https://www.wri.org/insights/roads-decoupling-21-countries-are-reducing-carbon-emissions-while-growing-gdp.

[88] United States Environmental Protection Agency. "Chart: How Average U.S. Vehicle CO2 Emissions Have Changed." *Inside Climate News*. April 2nd, 2018. https://insideclimatenews.org/infographics/chart-average-us-vehicle-co2-emissions/.

[89] Ibid.

[90] Corryn Wetzel. "This New Installation Pulled 20,000 Pounds of Plastic From the Great Pacific Garbage Patch." *Smithsonian Magazine*. Oct 19th, 2021. https://www.smithsonianmag.com/smart-news/this-new-installation-just-pulled-20000-pounds-of-plastic-from-the-great-pacific-garbage-patch-180978895/.

[91] "Oceans in danger: the threats they face." *United Nations*. June 8th, 2022. https://unric.org/en/oceans-in-danger-the-threats-they-face/#:~:text=According%20to%20the%20Food%20and,by%20ships%20along%20the%20seafloor.

[92] Scott Snowden. "New Enzyme Breaks Down Plastic In Hours And Enables High-Quality Recycling." *Forbes*. April 11, 2020. https://www.forbes.com/sites/scottsnowden/2020/04/11/new-enzyme-breaks-down-plastic-in-hours/?sh=11e43f685e4e.

[93] Ali Velshi. "The world could look "very different" thanks to this major fusion breakthrough." *MSNBC*. Dec 17th, 2022. https://www.msnbc.com/ali-velshi/watch/the-world-could-look-very-different-thanks-to-this-major-fusion-breakthrough-157981253844.

And, Gareth Willmer. "Major Breakthrough Puts Dream of Unlimited, Clean Nuclear Fusion Energy Within Reach." June 29th, 2022. https://scitechdaily.com/major-breakthrough-puts-dream-of-unlimited-clean-nuclear-fusion-energy-within-reach/.

[94] "Household air pollution." *World Health Organization*. July 27th, 2022. https://www.who.int/news-room/fact-sheets/detail/household-air-pollution-and-health.

[95] "extinction." *PBS*. https://www.pbs.org/wgbh/evolution/extinction/massext/index.html.

[96] "How Fracking Strengthens America." *Clear Path*. https://clearpath.org/tech-101/how-fracking-strengthens-america/#:~:text=Fracked%20natural%20gas%20burns%20more,world%20in%20reducing%20carbon%20pollution.&text=It%20may%20sound%20strange%2C%20but,been%20good%20for%20the%20climate.

[97] Umair Irfan. "The best case for and against a fracking ban." *Vox*. Oct 7th, 2020. https://www.vox.com/energy-and-environment/2019/9/12/20857196/kamala-fracking-ban-biden-climate-change.

[98] Jillian Ambrose. "Back the global fracking ban, campaigners urge UN." *The Guardian*. Sep 20th, 2019.

https://www.theguardian.com/environment/2019/sep/19/campaigners-urge-un-to-endorse-global-fracking-ban.

[99] Umair Irfan. "The best case for and against a fracking ban." *Vox*. Oct 7th, 2020. https://www.vox.com/energy-and-environment/2019/9/12/20857196/kamala-fracking-ban-biden-climate-change.

[100] Taisha Diaz. "Indigenous environmentalism." *The Indigenous Foundation*. https://www.theindigenousfoundation.org/articles/indigenous-environmentalism#:~:text=Indigenous%20Peoples%20see%20themselves%20as,and%20are%20respected%20as%20such.

[101] Too many individual pieces of evidence to cite. I'd encourage you to do a Google search of any of the aforementioned claims you're skeptical about. There's a proposal to ban just about anything for environmental reasons.

[102] Steven Pinker. *The Better Angels of Our Nature: Why Violence Has Declined*. Viking Press, a subsidiary of Penguin Books, New York, 2011.

[103] "Decline of Global Extreme Poverty Continues but Has Slowed: World Bank." *World Bank*. Sep 19th, 2018. https://www.worldbank.org/en/news/press-release/2018/09/19/decline-of-global-extreme-poverty-continues-but-has-slowed-world-bank.

[104] Navin Singh Khadka. "COP26: Did India betray vulnerable nations?." *BBC News*. Nov 16th, 2021. https://www.bbc.com/news/world-asia-india-59286790.

[105] Felicity Morse. "The pen, the sword and the Prophet." *BBC News*. Jan 13th, 2015. https://www.bbc.com/news/newsbeat-30803391.

[106] Christopher Nolan. *The Dark Knight*. Warner Bros. Pictures, FilmFlex. Released July 18th, 2008.

[107] Val Crofts. "Humble Statesman: How George Washington's Selfless Resignation Ensured Power Remained With the American People." *Constituting America*. https://constitutingamerica.org/humble-statesman-how-george-washingtons-selfless-resignation-ensured-power-remained-with-the-american-people-guest-essayist-val-crofts/.

[108] "Lucius Quinctius Cincinnatus." *Encyclopedia Britannica*. https://www.britannica.com/biography/Lucius-Quinctius-Cincinnatus.

[109] Reuters Fact Check. "Fact Check-'Test a man's character' quote misattributed to Abraham Lincoln." *Reuters*. Aug 3rd, 2021. https://www.reuters.com/article/factcheck-abrahamlincoln-power-idUSL1N2PA1V7.

And, Robert G. Ingersoll. "Motley and Monarch." *The North American* Review. New York. Vol. 141. Dec, 1885. p. 528-531.

[110] The origin of this quote is unknown, though it is said to be coined by Abbot Bernard of Clairvaux sometime in the mid 1100's.

[111] "Blue Zones." *Blue Zones*. https://www.bluezones.com/#.

[112] Dan Buettner. "Power 9®: Reverse Engineering Longevity." *Blue Zones*. https://www.bluezones.com/2016/11/power-9/.

[113] Erin Eatough. "What is ikigai and how can it change my life?." *Better Up*. May 7th, 2021. https://www.betterup.com/blog/what-is-ikigai#:~:text=Ikigai%20is%20a%20Japanese%20concept,out%20of%20bed%20every%20day.

[114] Jeffrey M. Jones. "U.S. Church Membership Falls Below Majority for First Time." *Gallup*. March 29th, 2021. https://news.gallup.com/poll/341963/church-membership-falls-below-majority-first-time.aspx#:~:text=U.S.%20church%20membership%20was%2073,2010%20and%2047%25%20in%202020.

[115] "MILLENNIAL MELANCHOLY: Nine in ten young Brits believe their life lacks purpose, according to shocking new study." *The Sun*. Aug 2nd, 2019. https://www.thesun.co.uk/news/9637619/young-brits-life-lacks-purpose/.

[116] Christie Hartman. "Loneliness Statistics (2022): By Country, Demographics & More." *The Roots of Loneliness Project*. May 24th, 2022. https://www.rootsofloneliness.com/loneliness-statistics#loneliness-worldwide.

[117] Robert Putnam. *Bowling Alone*. Simon & Schuster, New York, 2000.

[118] Jordan Gaines Lewis. "This is How the Brain Filters Out Unimportant Details." *Psychology Today*. Feb 11th, 2015. https://www.psychologytoday.com/ca/blog/brain-babble/201502/is-how-the-brain-filters-out-unimportant-details.

[119] Adam Halberstadt and Mark Geyer. "Do Psychedelics Expand the Mind by Reducing Brain Activity?." *Scientific American*. May 15th, 2012.

https://www.scientificamerican.com/article/do-psychedelics-expand-mind-reducing-brain-activity/.

And, Maia Szalavitz. "Magic Mushrooms Expand the Mind By Dampening Brain Activity." *TIME*. Jan 24, 2012. https://healthland.time.com/2012/01/24/magic-mushrooms-expand-the-mind-by-dampening-brain-activity/.

[120] Plato. *The Republic*. "Book VII." 514-517.

[121] "noumenon." *Encyclopedia Britannica*. https://www.britannica.com/topic/noumenon.

And, "phenomenon." *Encyclopedia Britannica*. https://www.britannica.com/topic/phenomenon-philosophy.

[122] Not an exact quote, but the origin of this sentiment seems to be ascribed to *The Diamond Sutra*. The same idea is expressed in commentary on *The Diamon Sutra*. Thich Nhat Hanh. *The Diamond That Cuts Through Illusion*. "Part One, Chapter Five, Signlessness." Parallax Press, 2006.

[123] Christopher F. Chabris and Daniel J. Simons. *The Invisible Gorilla: How Our Intuitions Deceive Us*. Crown Publishers, an imprint of Crown Publishing Group, a division of Random House, Inc,. New York, 2010.

And, http://www.theinvisiblegorilla.com/gorilla_experiment.html.

[124] Ashley Hamer. "The Double-Slit Experiment Cracked Reality Wide Open." *Discovery*. August 1st, 2019. https://www.discovery.com/science/Double-Slit-Experiment.

And, Marianne. "Physics in a minute: The double-slit experiment." *Plus*. Nov 19th, 2020. https://plus.maths.org/content/physics-minute-double-slit-experiment-0.

[125] Jeremy Bernstein. "Erwin Schrödinger." *Encyclopedia Britannica*. Last updated Jan 1st, 2023. https://www.britannica.com/biography/Erwin-Schrodinger.

[126] René Descartes. *Meditations of First Philosophy*. "Meditation II." First published in 1641.

[127] Aristotle. *Metaphysics*. "Book 12, part six."

[128] "The Big Bang." *Nasa Science*. https://science.nasa.gov/astrophysics/focus-areas/what-powered-the-big-bang.

[129] For those interested in the idea of a universe before the Big Bang that collapsed in on itself and an infinite cycle of universe creation, look into the Big Crunch Theory.

Eric Betz. "The Beginning to the End of the Universe: The Big Crunch vs. The Big Freeze." *Astronomy*. Jan 31st, 2021. https://astronomy.com/news/magazine/2021/01/the-beginning-to-the-end-of-the-universe-the-big-crunch-vs-the-big-freeze.

And, William Harris. "How the Big Crunch Theory Works." *How Stuff Works*. Feb 16th, 2021. https://science.howstuffworks.com/dictionary/astronomy-terms/big-crunch.htm.

[130] "physics (n.)." *Online Etymology Dictionary*. https://www.etymonline.com/word/physics.

[131] Hesiod. *Theogony*. "The First Gods." Verse 116-117.

[132] Robert W. Sterner, Gaston E. Small, and James M. Hood. "The Conservation of Mass." *Nature Education Knowledge*. 2011.

[133] "metaphysics (n.)." *Online Etymology Dictionary*. https://www.etymonline.com/word/metaphysics.

[134] A. David-Neel and Lama Yongden. English Translation by Capt. H. N. M. Hardy. *The Secret Oral Teachings in Tibetan Buddhist Sects*. Maha Bodhi Society of India, Calcutta, 1960.

[135] Ethan Siegel. "It Takes 26 Fundamental Constants To Give Us Our Universe, But They Still Don't Give Everything." *Forbes*. Aug 22nd, 2015. https://www.forbes.com/sites/ethansiegel/2015/08/22/it-takes-26-fundamental-constants-to-give-us-our-universe-but-they-still-dont-give-everything/?sh=3b594cab4b86.

[136] This is an idea seemingly of ancient origins, said by many. I first heard it used by Alan Watts, but this idea has also been expressed by Carl Sagan, Neil deGrasse Tyson, Deepak Chopra, and is a common sentiment among Indian philosophers.

[137] Alan Watts. *What is Life About?*. Speech extract in "The False Idea of Who You Are – Alan Watts." *YouTube*. Timestamp 3:33-3:45. Jun 8th, 2021. https://www.youtube.com/watch?v=4yaBJVfyy00&t=70s.

[138] Alan Watts. *Nature of Consciousness from Human Consciousness*. Speech extract in "The Real You – Alan Watts." *YouTube*. Timestamp 1:44-2:17. Aug 25th, 2012. https://www.youtube.com/watch?v=mMRrCYPxD0I&t=0s.

[139] "psychology (n.)." *Online Etymology Dictionary*. https://www.etymonline.com/word/psychology.

[140] "cosmology (n.)." *Online Etymology Dictionary*. https://www.etymonline.com/word/cosmology.

And "cosmos (n.)." *Online Etymology Dictionary*. https://www.etymonline.com/word/cosmos?ref=etymonline_crossreference.

[141] Holy Bible. Exodus 3:1-15.

[142] "atman." *Encyclopedia Britannica*. https://www.britannica.com/topic/atman.

And, "brahman." *Encyclopedia Britannica*. https://www.britannica.com/topic/brahman-Hindu-concept.

[143] "god (n.)." *Online Etymology Dictionary*. https://www.etymonline.com/word/god.

[144] Michael LeFebvre. "'I Am Who I Am'? The Real Meaning of God's Name in Exodus." *Center For Hebraic Thought*. Feb 15th, 2022. https://hebraicthought.org/meaning-of-gods-name-i-am-exodus/.

[145] The Mystical Experience Questionnaire (MEQ 30). *Trippingly*. Dec 24th, 2020. https://www.trippingly.net/lsd-studies/2018/5/22/the-mystical-experience-questionaire-30-questions.

[146] Allison Eck. "Altering Perception on Psychedelics: Growing evidence for the safety and efficacy of psychedelics could lead to better treatments for anxiety, depression, pain, and other often intractable conditions." *Harvard Medicine*. Spring 2022. https://hms.harvard.edu/magazine/viral-world/altering-perceptions-psychedelics.

And, The Johns Hopkins Center for Psychedelic and Consciousness Research. "Psychedelics Research and Psilocybin Therapy." Psychiatry and Behavioral Sciences. *Johns Hopkins Medicine*. https://www.hopkinsmedicine.org/psychiatry/research/psychedelics-research.html.

[147] The Gospel of Thomas, verse 113.

[148] "The power of the placebo effect." *Harvard Health Publishing*, a division of Harvard Medical School. Dec 13th, 2021. https://www.health.harvard.edu/mental-health/the-power-of-the-placebo-effect.

[149] Tony Robins, a common saying from his talks and books.

[150] "Mental Illness and Addiction: Facts and Statistics." *Centre For Addiction and Mental Health*. https://www.camh.ca/en/driving-change/the-crisis-is-real/mental-health-statistics.

[151] National Center for Health Statistics. "Leading Causes of Death." *Centers for Disease Control and Prevention*. Sep 6th, 2022. https://www.cdc.gov/nchs/fastats/leading-causes-of-death.htm.

[152] Attributed to Helen Hayes.

[153] Joseph Campbell. *The Hero With a Thousand Faces*. Pantheon Books, New York, 1949.

[154] Carl Jung. *Aion: Researches into the Phenomenology of the Self*. Chapter five. Princeton University Press, 1970, second edition. p. 43.

www.ingramcontent.com/pod-product-compliance
Lightning Source LLC
Chambersburg PA
CBHW030034100526
44590CB00011B/195